U.S. Fish & Wildlife Service

2011 National Survey of Fishing, Hunting, and Wildlife-Associated Recreation

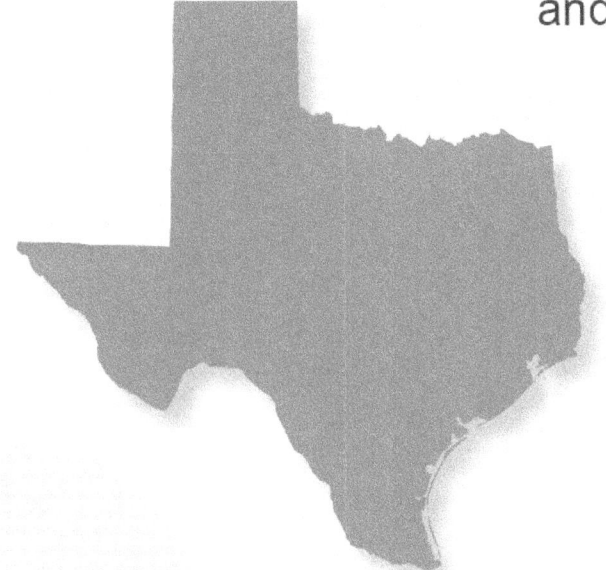

Texas

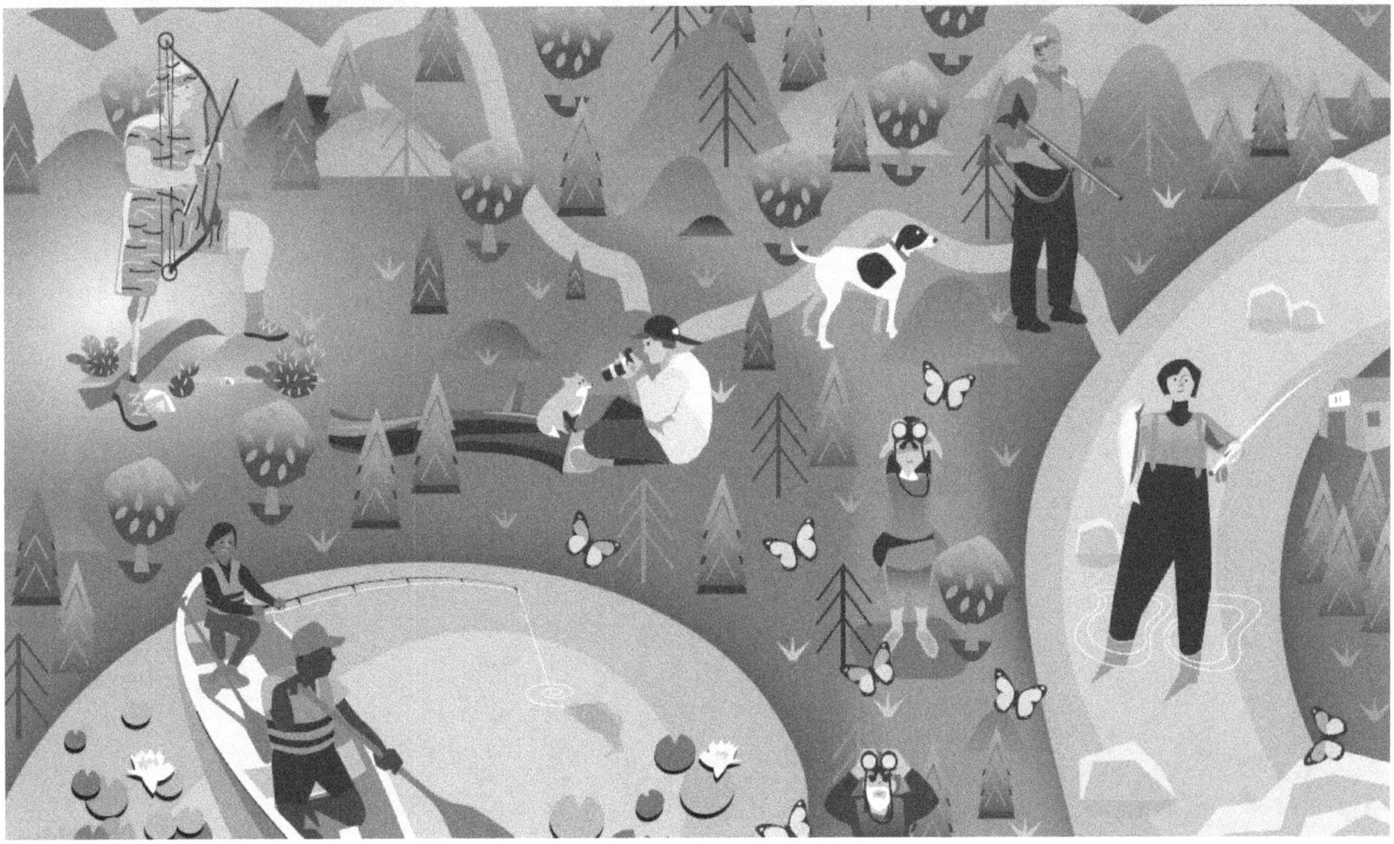

FHW/11-TX
Issued May 2013

2011 National Survey of
Fishing, Hunting, and
Wildlife-Associated Recreation

Texas

U.S. Department of the Interior
Sally Jewell,
Secretary

U.S. Fish and Wildlife Service
Dan Ashe,
Director

U.S. Department of Commerce
Rebecca M. Blank,
Acting Secretary

Economics and Statistics Administration
Mark Doms,
Under Secretary for Economic Affairs

U.S. CENSUS BUREAU
Thomas L. Mesenbourg,
Senior Adviser Performing the Duties
of the Director

ECONOMICS
AND STATISTICS
ADMINISTRATION

Economics and Statistics
Administration
Mark Doms,
Under Secretary for
Economic Affairs

U.S. CENSUS BUREAU
Thomas L. Mesenbourg,
Senior Adviser Performing the Duties
of the Director

U.S. Department of the Interior
Sally Jewell,
Secretary

U.S. Fish and Wildlife Service
Dan Ashe,
Director

Wildlife and Sport Fish Restoration
Hannibal Bolton,
Assistant Director

The U.S. Department of the Interior protects and manages the Nation's natural resources and cultural heritage; provides scientific and other information about those resources; and honors its trust responsibilities or special commitments to American Indians, Alaska Natives, and affiliated Island Communities. The mission of the Department's U.S. Fish and Wildlife Service is working with others to conserve, protect, and enhance fish, wildlife, and their habitats for the continuing benefit of the American people. The Service is responsible for national programs of vital importance to our natural resources, including administration of the Wildlife and Sport Fish Restoration Programs. These two programs provide financial assistance to the States for projects to enhance and protect fish and wildlife resources and to assure their availability to the public for recreational purposes. Multistate grants from these programs fund the National Survey of Fishing, Hunting, and Wildlife-Associated Recreation.

Suggested Citation

U.S. Department of the Interior, U.S. Fish and Wildlife Service, and U.S. Department of Commerce, U.S. Census Bureau. 2011 National Survey of Fishing, Hunting, and Wildlife-Associated Recreation.

Contents

List of Tables

Foreword

When I was growing up, it was taken as a matter of faith that kids belonged outside. I grew up with 4 brothers, and during those long, hot Atlanta summers, it was common for our mom to holler, "You boys get outside, and don't come back 'til it's dark." It never occurred to me or my brothers to do anything else in our spare time but explore the world around us. The truth is, we had little else to do. But those experiences – waking up on frosty mornings and starting the campfire, scanning trees for a shot at a scampering gray squirrel in the dawn light, scouring creek beds for crawdads and other fishing bait, or simply of the fun we had tramping through the forest – shaped who I am, and drew me to a career in conservation.

That's why I'm excited by this 2011 National Survey of Fishing, Hunting, and Wildlife-Associated Recreation. This report, the 12th in a series that began in 1955, documents a significant resurgence in the number of people embracing America's Great Outdoors. Hunting participation has increased by 9 percent, while angling participation grew by 11 percent. Nearly 38 percent of Americans participated in wildlife-related recreation, an increase of 2.6 million participants from the 2006 Survey.

In addition, wildlife-related recreation is a major driver of the nation's economy. The 2011 Survey estimates that Americans spent $145 billion on related gear, trips, licenses, land acquisition or leases, and other purchases, representing about one percent of the nation's gross domestic product. This spending creates thousands of jobs, supports countless local communities and provides vital funding for conservation.

This year marks the 75th anniversary of the Wildlife and Sport Fish Restoration Program, a cornerstone of wildlife conservation in the United States. Through excise taxes on firearms, ammunition, archery and angling equipment, the U.S. Fish and Wildlife Service has distributed over $14 billion for State and territorial wildlife conservation programs.

This report would not have been possible without the combined efforts of state wildlife agencies – which provided financial support through the Multi-State Conservation Grant Programs – the Association of Fish and Wildlife Agencies and a number of major national conservation organizations. We also owe our gratitude to the thousands of survey respondents from households across America. Because of you, this Survey is the nation's definitive wildlife-related recreation database and information source concerning participation and purchases associated with hunting, fishing and other forms of wildlife-associated recreation nationwide.

The Fish and Wildlife Service is dedicated to connecting people and families with nature. We are proud to celebrate the good news in this report, and we look forward to continuing progress as we work with the States, and all our partners and the public to help keep recreational fishing, hunting, and wildlife watching growing and going strong.

Dan Ashe
Director, U.S. Fish and Wildlife Service

Survey Background and Method

The National Survey of Fishing, Hunting, and Wildlife-Associated Recreation (Survey) has been conducted since 1955 and is one of the oldest and most comprehensive continuing recreation surveys. The Survey collects information on the number of anglers, hunters, and wildlife watchers, how often they participate, and how much they spend on their activities in the United States.

Preparations for the 2011 Survey began in 2008 when the Association of Fish and Wildlife Agencies (AFWA) asked the Fish and Wildlife Service to coordinate the twelfth National Survey of wildlife-related recreation. Funding came from the Multistate Conservation Grant Programs, authorized by Wildlife and Sport Fish Restoration Acts, as amended.

Four regional technical committees were set up under the auspices of AFWA to ensure that State fish and wildlife agencies had an opportunity to participate in all phases of survey planning and design. The committees were made up of agency representatives.

We consulted with State and Federal agencies and nongovernmental organizations such as the American Sportfishing Association and National Shooting Sports Foundation to determine survey content. Other sportspersons' organizations and conservation groups, industry representatives, and researchers also provided valuable advice.

Data collection for the Survey was carried out in two phases by the U.S. Census Bureau. The first phase was the screen which began in April 2011. During the screening phase, the Census Bureau interviewed a sample of 48,600 households nationwide, to determine who in the household had fished, hunted, or wildlife watched in 2010, and who had engaged or planned to engage in those activities in 2011. In most cases, one adult household member provided information for all members. The screen primarily covered 2010 activities while the next, more in-depth phase covered 2011 activities. For more information on the 2010 data, refer to Appendix B.

The second phase of data collection consisted of three detailed interview waves. The first wave began in April 2011 concurrent with the screen, the second in September 2011, and the last in January 2012. Interviews were conducted with samples of likely anglers, hunters, and wildlife watchers who were identified in the initial screening phase. Interviews were conducted primarily by telephone, with in-person interviews for respondents who could not be reached by phone. Respondents in the second survey phase were limited to those who were at least 16 years old. Each respondent provided information pertaining only to his or her activities and expenditures. Sample sizes were designed to provide statistically reliable results at the state level. Altogether, interviews were completed for 11,330 anglers and hunters and 9,329 wildlife watchers. More detailed information on sampling procedures and response rates is found in Appendix D.

Comparability With Previous Surveys

The 2011 Survey's questions and methodology were similar to those used in the 2006, 2001, 1996, and 1991 Surveys. Therefore, the estimates are comparable.

The methodology for these Surveys differs significantly from the 1955 to 1985 Surveys, so these estimates are not directly comparable to those of earlier surveys. Changes in methodology included reducing the recall period over which respondents had to report their activities and expenditures. Previous Surveys used a 12-month recall period which resulted in greater reporting bias. Research found that the amount of activity and expenditures reported in 12-month recall surveys was overestimated in comparison with that reported using shorter recall periods.

Highlights

Introduction

The National Survey of Fishing, Hunting, and Wildlife-Associated Recreation reports results from interviews with U.S. residents about their fishing, hunting, and wildlife watching. This report focuses on 2011 participation and expenditures of persons 16 years of age and older.

The Survey is a snapshot of one year. The information it collected tells us how many people participated and how much they spent on their activities in the State in 2011. It does not tell us how many anglers, hunters, and wildlife watchers there were because many do not participate every year. For example, based on information collected in the Survey's household screen phase, we can estimate that about 51 percent more anglers and 44 percent more hunters participated nationally in at least 1 of the 5 years prior to the screen survey year 2010.

In addition to 2011 estimates, we also provide trend information in the Highlights section and Appendix C of the report. The 2011 numbers reported can be compared with those in the 1991, 1996, 2001, and 2006 Survey reports because they used similar methodologies. The 2011 estimates should not be directly compared with results from Surveys conducted prior to 1991 because of changes in methodology to improve accuracy.

The report also provides information on participation in wildlife recreation in 2010, particularly of persons 6 to 15 years of age. The 2010 information is provided in Appendix B. Information about the Survey's scope and coverage is in Appendix D. The remainder of this section defines important terms used in the Survey.

This report does not provide information about the State's wildlife resources. That, and additional information on wildlife-related recreation, may be obtained from State fish and wildlife agencies. The Association of Fish and Wildlife Agencies can provide the addresses and telephone numbers of those agencies. The Association's website is www.fishwildlife.org.

Additionally, this report does not provide information about the State's number of licensed anglers and hunters. Historical license data can be found at wsfrprograms.fws.gov.

Wildlife-Related Recreation

Wildlife-related recreation is fishing, hunting, and wildlife-watching activities. These categories are not mutually exclusive because many individuals participated in more than one activity. Wildlife-related recreation is reported in two major categories: (1) fishing and hunting, and (2) wildlife watching, which includes observing, photographing, and feeding fish or wildlife.

Sportspersons

Anglers   Hunters

Fished   Fished   Hunted
only   and   only
            hunted

Fishing and Hunting

This Survey reports information about residents of the United States who fished or hunted in 2011, regardless of whether they were licensed. The fishing and hunting sections report information for three groups: (1) sportspersons, (2) anglers, and (3) hunters.

Sportspersons

Sportspersons are those who fished or hunted. Individuals who fished or hunted commercially in 2011 are reported as sportspersons *only* if they also fished or hunted for recreation. The sportspersons group is composed of the three subgroups shown in the diagram below: (1) those that fished and hunted, (2) those that only fished, and (3) those that only hunted.

The total number of sportspersons is equal to the sum of people who only fished, only hunted, and both hunted and fished. It is not the sum of all anglers and all hunters because those people who both fished and hunted are included in both the angler and hunter population and would be incorrectly counted twice.

Anglers

Anglers are sportspersons who only fished plus those who fished and hunted. Anglers include not only licensed hook and line anglers, but also those who have no license and those who use special methods such as fishing with spears. Three types of fishing are reported: (1) freshwater, excluding the Great Lakes, (2) Great Lakes, and (3) saltwater. Since many anglers participated in more than one type of fishing, the total number of anglers is less than the sum of the three types of fishing.

Hunters

Hunters are sportspersons who only hunted plus those who hunted and fished. Hunters include not only licensed hunters using rifles and shotguns, but also those who have no license and those who engage in hunting with archery equipment, muzzleloaders, other primitive firearms, or pistols or handguns.

Four types of hunting are reported: (1) big game, (2) small game, (3) migratory bird, and (4) other animals. Since many hunters participated in more than one type of hunting, the sum of hunters for big game, small game, migratory bird, and other animals exceeds the total number of hunters.

Wildlife Watchers

Since 1980, the National Survey has included information on wildlife-watching activities in addition to fishing and hunting. However, unlike the 1980 and 1985 Surveys, the National Surveys since 1991 have collected data only for those activities where the *primary* purpose was wildlife watching (observing, photographing, or feeding wildlife).

The 2011 Survey uses a strict definition of wildlife watching. Participants must either take a "special interest" in wildlife around their homes or take a trip for the "primary purpose" of wildlife watching. Secondary wildlife watching, such as incidentally observing wildlife while pleasure driving, is not included.

Two types of wildlife-watching activity are reported: (1) away-from-home (formerly nonresidential) activities and (2) around-the-home (formerly residential) activities. Because some people participated in more than one type of wildlife watching, the sum of participants in each type will be greater than the total number of wildlife watchers. Only those engaged in activities whose *primary* purpose was wildlife watching are included in the Survey. The two types of wildlife-watching activity are defined below.

Away-From-Home

This group includes persons who took trips or outings of at least 1 mile from home for the primary purpose of observing, feeding, or photographing fish and wildlife. Trips to fish or hunt or scout and trips to zoos, circuses, aquariums, and museums are not considered wildlife-watching activities.

Around-The-Home

This group includes those who participated within 1 mile of home and involves one or more of the following: (1) closely observing or trying to identify birds or other wildlife; (2) photographing wildlife; (3) feeding birds or other wildlife; (4) maintaining natural areas of at least 1/4 acre where benefit to wildlife is the primary concern; (5) maintaining plantings (shrubs, agricultural crops, etc.) where benefit to wildlife is the primary concern; or (6) visiting parks and natural areas within 1 mile of home for the primary purpose of observing, feeding, or photographing wildlife.

2011 Texas Summary

Activities in Texas by Residents and Nonresidents

Fishing

Anglers	**2,246,000**
Days of fishing	30,667,000
Average days per angler	14
Total expenditures	$1,540,434,000
Trip-related	$1,045,330,000
Equipment and other	$495,104,000
Average per angler	$667
Average trip expenditure per day	$34

Hunting

Hunters	**1,147,000**
Days of hunting	20,372,000
Average days per hunter	18
Total expenditures	$1,835,098,000
Trip-related	$837,479,000
Equipment and other	$997,619,000
Average per hunter	$1,592
Average trip expenditure per day	$41

Wildlife Watching

Total wildlife-watching participants	**4,376,000**
Away-from-home participants	1,026,000
Around-the-home participants	4,249,000
Days of participation away from home	11,840,000
Average days of participation away from home	12
Total expenditures	$1,823,758,000
Trip-related	$478,080,000
Equipment and other	$1,345,678,000
Average per participant	$413
Average trip expenditure per day	$40

Activities by Texas Residents Both Inside and Outside Texas

Fishing

Anglers	**2,355,000**
Days of fishing	34,710,000
Average days per angler	15
Total expenditures	$1,711,265,000
Trip-related	$1,217,961,000
Equipment and other	$493,304,000
Average per angler	$727
Average trip expenditure per day	$35

Hunting

Hunters	**1,080,000**
Days of hunting	19,848,000
Average days per hunter	18
Total expenditures	$1,696,128,000
Trip-related	$723,286,000
Equipment and other	$972,842,000
Average per hunter	$1,571
Average trip expenditure per day	$36

Wildlife Watching

Total wildlife-watching participants	**4,263,000**
Away-from-home participants	977,000
Around-the-home participants	4,249,000
Days of participation away from home	11,193,000
Average days of participation away from home	11
Total expenditures	$1,677,780,000
Trip-related	$335,013,000
Equipment and other	$1,342,767,000
Average per participant	$394
Average trip expenditure per day	$30

Wildlife-Related Recreation

Participation in Texas

The 2011 Survey found that 6.3 million Texas residents and nonresidents 16 years old and older fished, hunted, or wildlife watched in Texas. Of the total number of participants, 2.2 million fished, 1.1 million hunted, and 4.4 million participated in wildlife-watching activities, which includes observing, feeding, and photographing wildlife. The sum of anglers, hunters, and wildlife watchers exceeds the total number of participants in wildlife-related recreation because many of the individuals engaged in more than one wildlife-related activity.

Participation in 2011 by 6- to 15-Year-Old Texas Residents

The focus of the National Survey is on the activity of participants 16 years old and older. However, the activity of 6- to 15-year-olds can be calculated using the screening data covering the year 2010. It is assumed for estimation purposes that the proportion of 6- to 15-year-old participants to participants 16 years old and older remained the same in 2010 and 2011. Based on this assumption, in addition to the 2.4 million resident anglers 16 years old or older in Texas, there were 523 thousand resident anglers 6 to 15 years old. Also, there were 1.1 million Texans 16 years old and older and 147 thousand Texans 6 to 15 years old who hunted. Finally, there were 4.3 million Texans 16 years old and older and 961 thousand Texans 6 to 15 years old who wildlife watched. Information on 2010 data for 6- to 15-year-olds is provided in Appendix B.

Expenditures in Texas

In 2011, state residents and nonresidents spent $6.2 billion on wildlife recreation in Texas. Of that total, trip-related expenditures were $2.4 billion and equipment expenditures totaled $2.9 billion. The remaining $994 million was spent on licenses, contributions, land ownership and leasing, and other items.

Percent of Total Participants by Activity
(Total: 6.3 million participants)

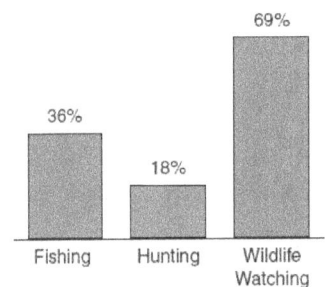

Percent of Total Residential Participants 6 to 15 Years Old by Activity: 2010
(Total: 1.4 million participants)

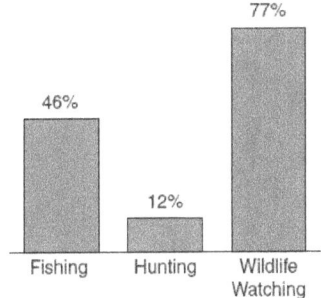

Participants in Wildlife-Related Recreation in Texas: 2011
(U.S. residents 16 years old and older)

Total	**6.3 million**
Sportspersons	
Total	**2.7 million**
Anglers...	2.2 million
Hunters...	1.1 million
Wildlife Watchers	
Total	**4.4 million**
Away from home	1.0 million
Around the home	4.2 million

Note: Detail does not add to total because of multiple responses

Source: Tables 1 and 24

Wildlife-Related Recreation Expenditures in Texas
(Total: $6.2 billion)

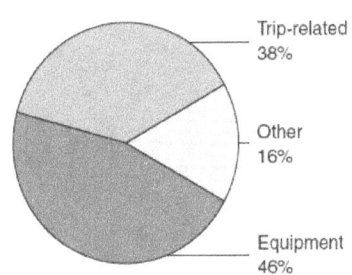

Sportspersons

In 2011, 2.7 million state resident and nonresident sportspersons 16 years old and older fished or hunted in Texas. This group was comprised of 2.2 million anglers (83 percent of all sportspersons) and 1.1 million hunters (42 percent of all sportspersons). Among the 2.7 million sportspersons who fished or hunted in the state, 1.6 million (58 percent) fished but did not hunt in Texas. Another 467 thousand (17 percent) hunted but did not fish there. The remaining 680 thousand (25 percent) fished and hunted in Texas in 2011.

Sportspersons' Participation in Texas
(State residents and nonresidents 16 years old and older)

Sportspersons (fished or hunted)	**2.7 million**
Anglers	**2.2 million**
Fished only	1.6 million
Fished and hunted	680 thousand
Hunters	**1.1 million**
Hunted only	467 thousand
Hunted and fished	680 thousand

Note: Detail does not add to total because of multiple responses

Source: Table 1

Anglers

Participants and Days of Fishing

In 2011, 2.2 million state residents and nonresidents 16 years old and older fished in Texas. Of this total, 2.1 million anglers (95 percent) were state residents and 114 thousand anglers (5 percent) were nonresidents. Anglers fished a total of 30.7 million days in Texas—an average of 14 days per angler. State residents fished 29.6 million days—96 percent of all fishing days in Texas. Nonresidents fished 1.1 million days in Texas—4 percent of all fishing days in the state.

A large majority of Texas residents who fished anywhere in the United States did so in their resident state. There were 2.4 million Texas residents 16 years old and older who fished in the United States in 2011 for a total of 34.7 million days. An estimated 91 percent of all Texas residents who fished did so in their home state. Of all fishing days by Texas residents, 85 percent or 29.6 million were in their home state. For further details about fishing in Texas, see Table 3.

Anglers in Texas
(State residents and nonresidents 16 years old and older)

Anglers	**2.2 million**
Residents	2.1 million
Nonresidents	114 thousand
Days of fishing	**30.7 million**
Residents	29.6 million
Nonresidents	1.1 million

Source: Table 3

In State/Out of State
(State residents 16 years old and older)

Texas anglers	**2.4 million**
In Texas	2.1 million
In other states	523 thousand
Days of fishing	**34.7 million**
In Texas	29.6 million
In other states	5.2 million

Note: Detail does not add to total because of multiple responses
Source: Table 3

Fishing Expenditures in Texas

All fishing-related expenditures in Texas totaled $1.5 billion in 2011. Trip-related expenditures, including food and lodging, transportation, and other expenses totaled $1.0 billion—68 percent of all fishing expenditures. Expenditures for food and lodging were $423 million and transportation expenditures were $298 million. Other trip expenses, such as equipment rental, bait, and cooking fuel, totaled $325 million. Each angler spent an average of $459 on trip-related costs during 2011.

Anglers spent $471 million on equipment in Texas in 2011, 31 percent of all fishing expenditures. Fishing equipment (rods, reels, lines, etc.) spending totaled $204 million—43 percent of the equipment total. Auxiliary equipment expenditures (tents, special fishing clothing, etc.) and special equipment expenditures (boats, vans, etc.) amounted to $267 million—57 percent of the equipment total. Expenditures classified as special and auxiliary equipment are on items that were purchased for fishing but could be used in activities other than fishing.

The purchase of other items, such as magazines, membership dues, licenses, permits, stamps, and land leasing and ownership, amounted to $24 million—2 percent of all fishing expenditures. For more details about fishing expenditures in Texas, see Tables 19 and 21 through 23.

Fishing Expenditures in Texas
(State residents and nonresidents 16 years old and older)

Total	**$1.5 billion**
Trip-related	$1.0 billion
Equipment	$471 million
Fishing	$204 million
Auxiliary and special	$267 million
Other	$24 million

Source: Table 19

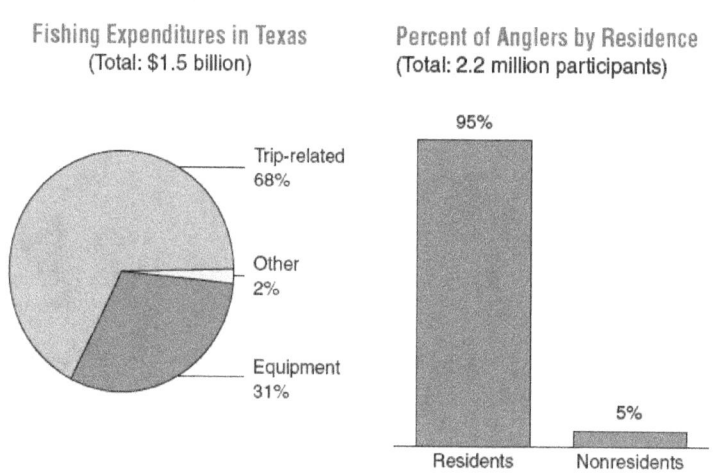

Fishing Expenditures in Texas
(Total: $1.5 billion)

Trip-related 68%
Other 2%
Equipment 31%

Percent of Anglers by Residence
(Total: 2.2 million participants)

95%
5%
Residents   Nonresidents

Comparative Fishing Expenditures by Type of Fishing

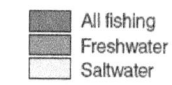

All fishing
Freshwater
Saltwater

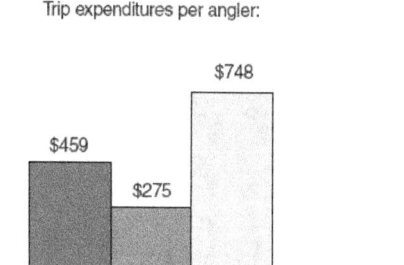

Trip expenditures per angler:

$459
$275
$748

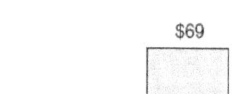

Trip expenditures per day:

$34
$21
$69

Hunters

Participants and Days of Hunting

In 2011, there were 1.1 million residents and nonresidents 16 years old and older who hunted in Texas. Resident hunters numbered 1.1 million, accounting for 94 percent of the hunters in Texas. There were 67 thousand nonresidents who hunted in Texas—6 percent of the State's hunters. Residents and nonresidents hunted 20.4 million days in 2011, an average of 18 days per hunter. Residents hunted 19.8 million days in Texas or 97 percent of all hunting days, while nonresidents spent 594 thousand days in Texas or 3 percent of all hunting days.

There were 1.1 million Texas residents 16 years old and older who hunted in the United States in 2011 for a total of 19.8 million days. An estimated 100 percent of all Texas residents who hunted did so in their home state. Of all hunting days by Texas residents, nearly 100 percent or 19.8 million were spent pursuing game in their home state. For further information on hunting activities by Texas residents, see Table 3.

Hunters in Texas
(State residents and nonresidents 16 years old and older)

Hunters	**1.1 million**
Residents	1.1 million
Nonresidents	67 thousand
Days of hunting	**20.4 million**
Residents	19.8 million
Nonresidents	594 thousand

Source: Table 3

In State/Out of State
(State residents 16 years old and older)

Texas hunters	**1.1 million**
In Texas	1.1 million
In other states	...
Days of hunting	**19.8 million**
In Texas	19.8 million
In other states	...

... Sample size too small (less than 10) to report data reliably
Source: Table 3

Hunting Expenditures in Texas

All hunting-related expenditures in Texas totaled $1.8 billion in 2011. Trip-related expenses, such as food and lodging, transportation, and other trip expenses, totaled $837 million—46 percent of total expenditures. Expenditures for food and lodging were $332 million and transportation expenditures were $379 million. Other trip expenses, such as equipment rental, totaled $126 million for the year. The average trip-related expenditure per hunter was $730.

Hunters spent $538 million on equipment—29 percent of all hunting expenditures. Hunting equipment (guns, ammunition, etc.) totaled $344 million and made up 64 percent of all equipment costs. Hunters spent $194 million on auxiliary equipment (tents, special hunting clothes, etc.) and special equipment (boats, vans, etc.), accounting for 36 percent of total equipment expenditures for hunting. Expenditures classified as special and auxiliary equipment are on items that were purchased for hunting but could be used in activities other than hunting.

The purchase of other items, such as magazines, membership dues, licenses, permits, and land leasing, and ownership, cost hunters $460 million—25 percent of all hunting expenditures. For more details on hunting expenditures in Texas, see Tables 20 through 23.

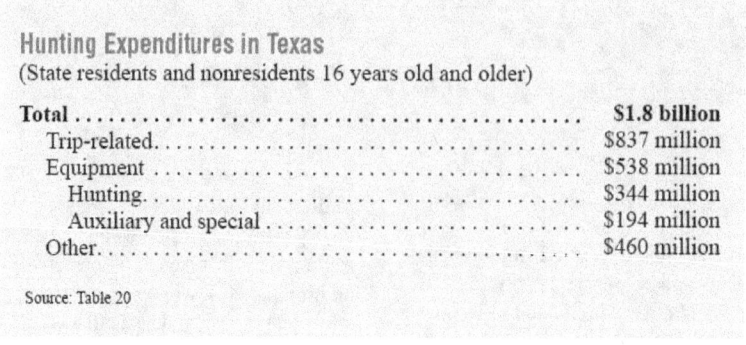

Hunting Expenditures in Texas
(State residents and nonresidents 16 years old and older)

Total	**$1.8 billion**
Trip-related	$837 million
Equipment	$538 million
Hunting	$344 million
Auxiliary and special	$194 million
Other	$460 million

Source: Table 20

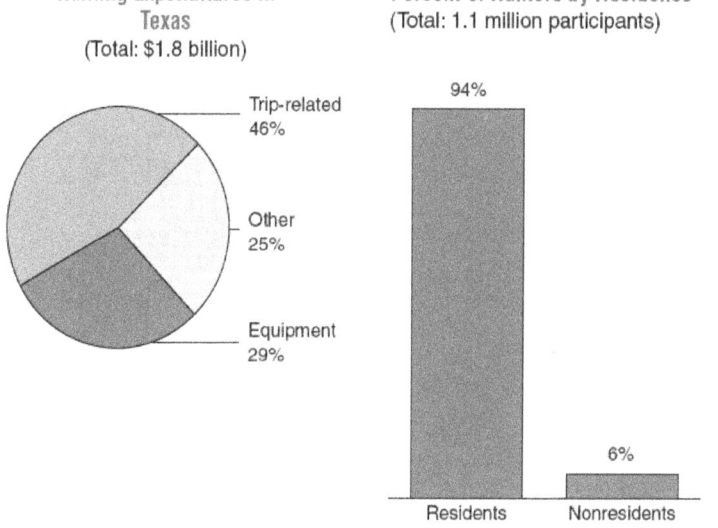

Hunting Expenditures in Texas
(Total: $1.8 billion)

Percent of Hunters by Residence
(Total: 1.1 million participants)

Comparative Hunting Expenditures by Type of Hunting

- All hunting
- Big game
- Small game
- Migratory birds
- Other animals

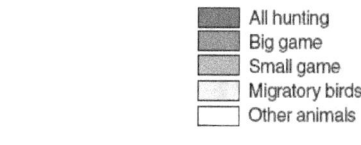

Trip expenditures per hunter:

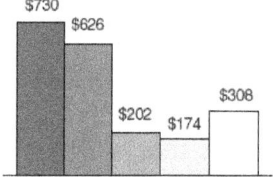

Trip expenditures per day:

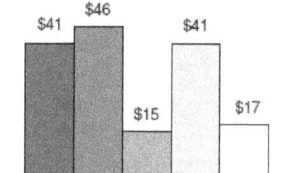

Wildlife Watchers

Participants and Days of Activity

In 2011, 4.4 million U.S. residents 16 years old and older fed, observed, or photographed wildlife in Texas. Most of them, 97 percent (4.2 million), enjoyed their activities close to home and are called "around-the-home" participants. Those persons who enjoyed wildlife at least one mile from home are called "away-from-home" participants. People participating in away-from-home activities in Texas in 2011 numbered 1.0 million—23 percent of all wildlife watchers in Texas. Of the 1.0 million, 899 thousand were state residents and 127 thousand were nonresidents.

Texans 16 years old and older who enjoyed away-from-home wildlife watching within their state totaled 899 thousand. Of this group, 899 thousand participants observed wildlife, 630 thousand fed wildlife, and 410 thousand photographed wildlife. Since some individuals engaged in more than one of the away-from-home activities during the year, the sum of wildlife observers, feeders, and photographers exceeds the total number away-from-home participants.

Texans spent 10.4 million days engaged in away-from-home wildlife-watching activities in their state. They spent 8.6 million days observing and 7.3 million days feeding wildlife. For further details about away-from-home activities, see Table 25.

Texas residents also took an active interest in wildlife around their homes. In 2011, 4.2 million state residents enjoyed observing, feeding, and photographing wildlife within one mile of their homes. Among this around-the-home group, 3.4 million fed, 3.2 million observed, and 1.5 million photographed wildlife around their homes. Another 493 thousand participants maintained natural areas of one-quarter acre or more for wildlife; 692 thousand participants maintained plantings for the benefit of wildlife; and 428 thousand participants visited parks or natural areas within a mile of home because of the wildlife. Summing the number of participants in these six activities results in an estimate that exceeds the total number of around-the-home participants because many people participated in more than one type of around-the-home activity. In addition, 23 percent of Texan around-the-home wildlife watchers also enjoyed wildlife away from home. For further details about Texas residents participating in around-the-home wildlife-watching activities, see Table 27.

Wildlife-Watching Participants in Texas
(State residents and nonresidents 16 years old and older)

Total	**4.4 million**
Around the home	4.2 million
Away from home	1.0 million

Note: Detail does not add to total because of multiple responses
Source: Table 24

Away-From-Home Wildlife-Watching Participation in Texas
(State residents and nonresidents 16 years old and older)

Participants, total	**1.0 million**
Observe wildlife	1.0 million
Photograph wildlife	519 thousand
Feed wildlife	651 thousand
Days, total	**11.8 million**
Observe wildlife	9.8 million
Photograph wildlife	3.8 million
Feed wildlife	8.0 million

Note: Detail does not add to total because of multiple responses
Source: Table 25

Around-The-Home Wildlife-Watching Participation in Texas
(State residents 16 years old and older)

Total	**4.2 million**
Feed wildlife	3.4 million
Observe wildlife	3.2 million
Photograph wildlife	1.5 million
Maintain natural areas	493 thousand
Maintain plantings	692 thousand
Visit parks and natural areas	428 thousand

Note: Detail does not add to total because of multiple responses
Source: Table 27

Wild Bird Observers

Bird watching attracted many wildlife enthusiasts in Texas. In 2011, 2.2 million people observed birds around the home and on trips in the state. A majority, 91 percent (2.0 million), observed wild birds around the home while 39 percent (879 thousand) took trips away from home to watch birds.

Wildlife-Watching Expenditures in Texas

Wildlife watchers spent $1.8 billion on wildlife-watching activities in Texas in 2011. Trip-related expenditures, including food and lodging ($254 million), transportation ($197 million), and other trip expenses ($28 million), such as equipment rental, amounted to $478 million. This summation comprised 26 percent of all wildlife-watching expenditures by participants. The average of the trip-related expenditures for away-from-home participants was $463 per person in 2011.

Wildlife-watching participants spent nearly $920 million on equipment—50 percent of all their expenditures. Specifically, wildlife-watching equipment (binoculars, special clothing, etc.) expenditures totaled $590 million, 64 percent of the equipment total. Auxiliary equipment expenditures (tents, backpacking equipment, etc.) and special equipment expenditures (campers, trucks, etc.) amounted to $330 million—36 percent of all equipment costs. Expenditures classified as special and auxiliary equipment are on items that were purchased for wildlife-watching recreation but could be used in activities other than wildlife watching.

Other items purchased by wildlife-watching participants, such as magazines, membership dues and contributions, land leasing and ownership, and plantings, totaled $426 million—23 percent of all wildlife-watching expenditures. For more details about wildlife-watching expenditures in Texas, see Table 31.

Wild Bird Observers in Texas
(State residents and nonresidents 16 years old and older)

Participants, total	**2.2 million**
Around the home	2.0 million
Away from home	879 thousand
Days, total	**295.3 million**
Around the home	286.2 million
Away from home	9.1 million

Note: Detail does not add to total because of multiple responses
Source: Table 29

Wildlife-Watching Expenditures in Texas
(State residents and nonresidents 16 years old and older)

Total	**$1.8 billion**
Trip-related	$478 million
Equipment	$920 million
Wildlife watching	$590 million
Auxiliary and special	$330 million
Other	$426 million

Source: Table 31

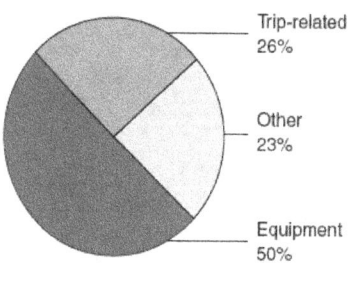

Wildlife-Watching
Expenditures in Texas
(Total: $1.8 billion)

Trip-related 26%
Other 23%
Equipment 50%

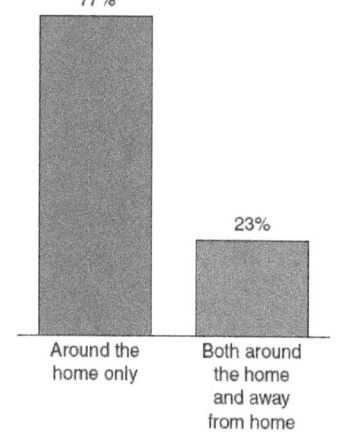

Away-From-Home Activity
by Around-The-Home Participants
(Total: 4.2 million participants)

77% — Around the home only
23% — Both around the home and away from home

2001–2011 Comparison

Comparing the estimates from the 2001, 2006, and 2011 Surveys gives a perspective on the state of wildlife-related recreation in the early twenty-first century in Texas. Only the most general recreation comparisons are presented here.

The best way to compare estimates from surveys is not to compare the estimates themselves but to compare the confidence intervals around the esti-mates. A 90-percent confidence interval around the estimate gives the range of estimates that 90 percent of all possible representative samples would supply. If the 90-percent confidence intervals of the two surveys' estimates overlap, it is not possible to say the two estimates are statistically different.

The state resident estimates cover the participation and expenditure activity of Texas residents anywhere in the United States. The in-state estimates cover the participation, day, and expenditure activity if U.S. residents in Texas.

The expenditure estimates were made comparable by adjusting the estimates for inflation—all estimates are in 2011 dollars.

Texas 2001 and 2011 Comparison
(Numbers in thousands. Expenditures in 2011 dollars)

	2001	2011	Percent change
Fishing			
Anglers in state	2,372	2,246	NS–5
Days in state	32,823	30,667	NS–7
In-state expenditures by U.S. anglers	$2,477,888	$1,540,434	–38
State resident anglers	2,381	2,355	NS–1
Total expenditures by state residents	$2,705,264	$1,711,265	NS–37
Hunting			
Hunters in state	1,201	1,147	NS–4
Days in state	14,081	20,372	NS45
In-state expenditures by U.S. hunters	$1,922,817	$1,835,098	NS–5
State resident hunters	1,126	1,080	NS–4
Total expenditures by state residents	$1,863,315	$1,696,128	NS–9
Away-From-Home Wildlife Watching			
Participants in state	1,002	1,026	NS2
Days in state	7,711	11,840	NS54
State resident participants	1,043	977	NS–6
Around-The-Home Wildlife Watching			
Total participants	2,930	4,249	45
Observers	2,050	3,197	56
Feeders	2,528	3,401	35
Wildlife-Watching Expenditures			
In-state expenditures by U.S. wildlife watchers	$1,629,497	$1,823,758	NS12
Total expenditures by state residents	$2,225,599	$1,677,780	NS–25

NS Not different from zero at the 10 percent level of significance

Texas 2006 and 2011 Comparison
(Numbers in thousands. Expenditures in 2011 dollars)

	2006	2011	Percent change
Fishing			
Anglers in state	2,527	2,246	NS−11
Days in state	41,141	30,667	−25
In-state expenditures by U.S. anglers	$3,611,980	$1,540,434	−57
State resident anglers	2,344	2,355	0
Total expenditures by state residents	$3,489,119	$1,711,265	−51
Hunting			
Hunters in state	1,101	1,147	NS4
Days in state	14,050	20,372	NS45
In-state expenditures by U.S. hunters	$2,479,571	$1,835,098	NS−26
State resident hunters	996	1,080	NS8
Total expenditures by state residents	$2,285,843	$1,696,128	NS−26
Away-From-Home Wildlife Watching			
Participants in state	956	1,026	NS7
Days in state	13,120	11,840	NS−10
State resident participants	1,176	977	NS−17
Around-The-Home Wildlife Watching			
Total participants	3,861	4,249	NS10
Observers	2,252	3,197	42
Feeders	3,332	3,401	NS2
Wildlife-Watching Expenditures			
In-state expenditures by U.S. wildlife watchers . . .	$3,279,265	$1,823,758	−44
Total expenditures by state residents	$3,861,985	$1,677,780	NS−57

NS Not different from zero at the 10 percent level of significance

Number of People Who Hunted and Fished in Texas: 2001–2011 (In thousands)

Number of People Who Wildlife Watched in Texas: 2001–2011 (In thousands)

Total Expenditures by Participants in Texas (In millions of 2011 dollars)

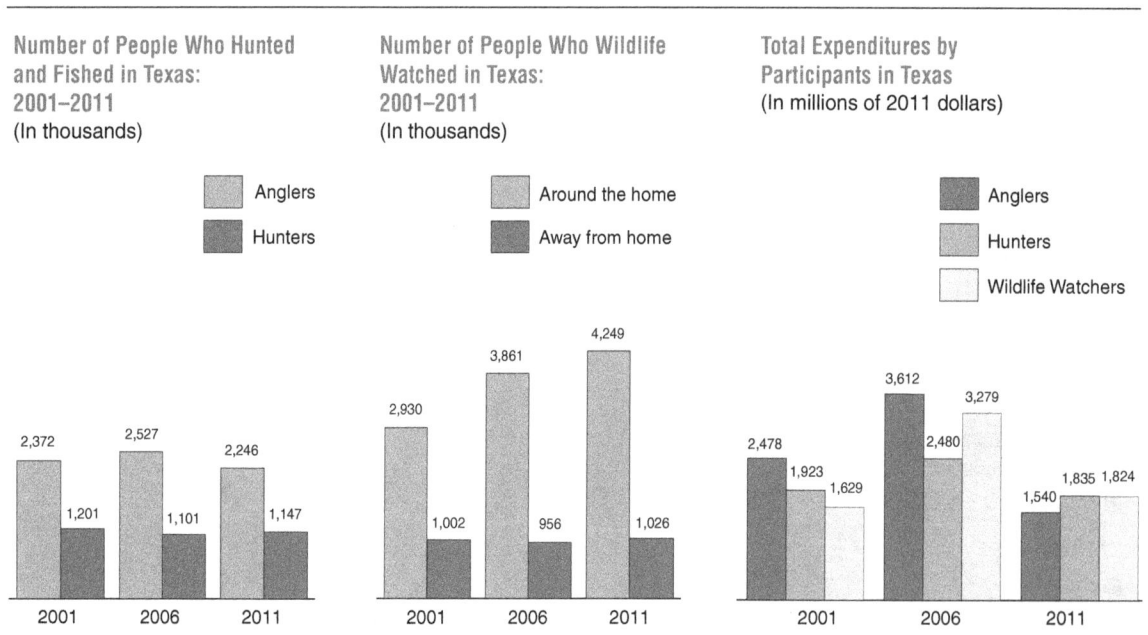

Tables

Guide to Statistical Tables

Purpose and Coverage of Tables

The statistical tables of this report were designed to meet a wide range of needs for those interested in wildlife-related recreation. Special terms used in these tables are defined in Appendix A.

The tables are based on responses to the 2011 Survey, which was designed to collect data about participation in wildlife-related recreation. To have taken part in the Survey, a respondent must have been a U.S. resident (a resident of one of the 50 states or the District of Columbia). No one residing outside the United States (including U.S. citizens) was eligible for interviewing. Therefore, reported state and national totals do not include participation by those who were not U.S. residents or who were U.S. citizens residing outside the United States.

Comparability With Previous Surveys

The numbers reported can be compared with those in the 1991, 1996, 2001, and 2006 Survey Reports. The methodology used in 2011 was similar to that used in those Surveys. These results should not be directly compared to results from Surveys earlier than 1991 since there were major changes in methodology. These changes were made to improve accuracy in the information provided.

Coverage of an Individual Table

Since the Survey covers many activities in various places by participants of different ages, all table titles, headnotes, stubs, and footnotes are designed to identify and articulate each item being reported in the table. For example, the title of Table 2 shows that data about anglers and hunters, their days of participation, and their number of trips are reported by type of activity. By contrast, the title of Table 7 indicates that it contains data on freshwater anglers and the days they fished for different species.

Percentages Reported in the Tables

Percentages are reported in the tables for the convenience of the user. When exclusive groups are being reported, the base of a percentage is apparent from its context because the percents add to 100 percent (plus or minus a rounding error). For example, Table 2 reports the number of trips taken by big game hunters, those taken by small game hunters, those taken by migratory bird hunters, and those taken by hunters pursuing other animals. These comprise 100 percent because they are exclusive categories.

Percents should not add to 100 when nonexclusive groups are being reported. Using Table 2 as an example again, note that adding the percentages associated with the total number of big game hunters, total small game hunters, total migratory bird hunters, and total hunters of other animals will not yield total hunters because respondents could hunt for more than one type of game.

When the base of the percentage is not apparent in context, it is identified in a footnote. For example, Table 15 reports two percentages with different bases: one base being the number of total participants at the head of the column and the other base being the total population who are described by the row category. Footnotes are used to clarify the bases of the reported percentages.

Footnotes to the Tables

Footnotes are used to clarify the information or items that are being reported in a table. Symbols in the body of a table indicate important footnotes. The following symbols are used in the tables to refer to the same footnote each time they appear:

* Estimate based on a sample size of 10–29.

... Sample size too small to report data reliably.

Z Less than 0.5 percent.

X Not applicable.

NA Not available.

Estimates based upon fewer than ten responses are regarded as being based on a sample size that is too small for reliable reporting. An estimate based upon at least 10 but fewer than 30 responses is treated as an estimate based on a small sample size. Other footnotes appear, as necessary, to qualify or clarify the estimates reported in the tables. In addition, these two important footnotes appear frequently:

- Detail does not add to total because of multiple responses.

- Detail does not add to total because of multiple responses and nonresponse.

"Multiple responses" is a term used to reflect the fact that individuals or their characteristics fall into more than one category. Using Table 5 as an example, those who fished in saltwater and freshwater appear in both of these totals. Yet each angler is represented only once in the "Total, all fishing" row. Similarly, in Table 12, those who hunt for big game and small game are counted only once as a hunter in the "Total, all hunting" row. Therefore, totals will be smaller than the sum of subcategories when multiple responses exist.

"Nonresponse" exists because the Survey questions were answered voluntarily, and some respondents did not or could not answer all the questions.

Table 1. Fishing and Hunting in Texas by Resident and Nonresident Sportspersons: 2011

(Population 16 years old and older. Numbers in thousands)

Sportspersons	Total, state residents and nonresidents		State residents		Nonresidents	
	Number	Percent of sportspersons	Number	Percent of resident sportspersons	Number	Percent of nonresident sportspersons
Total sportspersons (fished or hunted)	2,713	100	2,549	100	164	100
Total anglers	2,246	83	2,133	84	*114	*69
Fished only	1,566	58	1,469	58	*97	*59
Fished and hunted	680	25	664	26		
Total hunters	1,147	42	1,080	42	*67	*41
Hunted only	467	17	*416	*16	*51	*31
Hunted and fished	680	25	664	26		

* Estimate based on a sample size of 10–29   ... Sample size too small (less than 10) to report data reliably

Note: Detail does not add to total because of multiple responses

Table 2. Anglers and Hunters, Days of Participation, and Trips in Texas by Type of Fishing and Hunting: 2011

(Population 16 years old and older. Numbers in thousands)

Type of fishing and hunting	Participants		Days of participation		Trips	
	Number	Percent	Number	Percent	Number	Percent
FISHING						
Total, all fishing.........................	2,246	100	30,667	100	23,001	100
Total, all freshwater	1,758	78	22,616	74	17,798	77
Freshwater, except Great Lakes	1,758	78	22,616	74	17,798	77
Great Lakes	(X)	(X)	(X)	(X)	(X)	(X)
Saltwater	751	33	8,157	27	5,203	23
HUNTING						
Total, all hunting........................	1,147	100	20,372	100	19,956	100
Big game	937	82	12,651	62	9,516	48
Small game	*247	*22	*3,238	*16	*3,709	*19
Migratory birds	*391	*34	*1,672	*8	*1,632	*8
Other animals	432	38	7,882	39	5,099	26

* Estimate based on a sample size of 10–29   (X) Not applicable

Note: Detail does not add to total because of multiple responses

Table 3. Anglers and Hunters, Trips, and Days of Participation: 2011

(Population 16 years old and older. Numbers in thousands)

Anglers and hunters, trips and days of participation	Activity in Texas						Activity by Texas residents in United States					
	Total, state residents and nonresidents		State residents		Nonresidents		Total, in state of residence and in other states		In state of residence		In other states	
	Number	Percent	Number	Percent	Number	Percent	Number	Percent	Number	Percent	Number	Percent
FISHING												
Total anglers	2,246	100	2,133	95	*114	*5	2,355	100	2,133	91	*523	*22
Total trips	23,001	100	22,347	97	*654	*3	23,020	100	22,347	97	*673	*3
Total days of fishing	30,667	100	29,572	96	*1,095	*4	34,710	100	29,572	85	*5,163	*15
Average days of fishing	14	(X)	14	(X)	*10	(X)	15	(X)	14	(X)	*10	(X)
HUNTING												
Total hunters	1,147	100	1,080	94	*67	*6	1,080	100	1,080	100		
Total trips	19,956	100	19,233	96	*724	*4	19,287	100	19,233	100		
Total days of hunting	20,372	100	19,778	97	*594	*3	19,848	100	19,778	100		
Average days of hunting	18	(X)	18	(X)	*9	(X)	18	(X)	18	(X)		(X)

* Estimate based on a sample size of 10–29   ... Sample size too small (less than 10) to report data reliably   (X) Not applicable

Note: Detail does not add to total because of multiple responses

Table 4. Texas Resident Anglers and Hunters by Place Fished or Hunted: 2011

(Population 16 years old and older. Numbers in thousands)

Place fished or hunted	Anglers		Hunters	
	Number	Percent	Number	Percent
Total, all places	**2,355**	**100**	**1,080**	**100**
In-state only	1,831	78	1,049	97
In-state and other states	*301	*13		
In other states only	*222	*9		

* Estimate based on a sample size of 10–29   ... Sample size too small (less than 10) to report data reliably

Note: Detail does not add to total because of multiple responses and nonresponse

Table 5. Texas Resident Anglers and Hunters, Days of Participation, and Trips in the United States by Type of Fishing and Hunting: 2011

(Population 16 years old and older. Numbers in thousands)

Type of fishing and hunting	Participants		Days of participation		Trips	
	Number	Percent	Number	Percent	Number	Percent
FISHING						
Total, all fishing........................	**2,355**	**100**	**34,710**	**100**	**23,020**	**100**
Total, all freshwater	1,895	80	26,895	77	17,802	77
Freshwater, except Great Lakes	1,895	80	26,895	77	17,802	77
Great Lakes						
Saltwater	894	38	7,928	23	5,217	23
HUNTING						
Total, all hunting........................	**1,080**	**100**	**19,848**	**100**	**19,287**	**100**
Big game	893	83	12,237	62	9,067	47
Small game	*251	*23	*3,356	*17	*3,683	*19
Migratory birds	*379	*35	*1,611	*8	*1,611	*8
Other animals	*421	*39	*7,588	*38	*4,925	*26

* Estimate based on a sample size of 10–29   ... Sample size too small (less than 10) to report data reliably

Note: Detail does not add to total because of multiple responses

Table 6. Freshwater Anglers, Trips, Days of Fishing, and Type of Water Fished: 2011

(Population 16 years old and older. Numbers in thousands)

Anglers, trips, and days of fishing	Activity in Texas					
	Total, state residents and nonresidents		State residents		Nonresidents	
	Number	Percent	Number	Percent	Number	Percent
Total anglers	1,758	100	1,666	95	*92	*5
Total trips...	17,798	100	17,465	98	*333	*2
Total days of fishing	22,616	100	22,099	98	*518	*2
Average days of fishing	13	(X)	13	(X)	*6	(X)
ANGLERS						
Total, all types of water............................	1,758	100	1,666	95	*92	*5
Ponds, lakes, or reservoirs	1,640	100	1,549	94	*91	*6
Rivers or streams	*390	*100	*341	*87		
DAYS						
Total, all types of water............................	22,616	100	22,099	98	*518	*2
Ponds, lakes, or reservoirs	21,016	100	20,611	98	*405	*2
Rivers or streams	*3,708	*100	*3,563	*96		

* Estimate based on a sample size of 10–29   ... Sample size too small (less than 10) to report data reliably   (X) Not applicable

Note: Detail does not add to total because of multiple responses

Table 7. Freshwater Anglers and Days of Fishing in Texas by Type of Fish: 2011

(Population 16 years old and older. Numbers in thousands)

Anglers and days of fishing	Activity in Texas						
	Total, state residents and nonresidents			State residents		Nonresidents	
	Number	Percent of total types	Percent of anglers/days	Number	Percent of anglers/days	Number	Percent of anglers/days
ANGLERS							
Total, all types of fish	1,758	100	100	1,666	95	*92	*5
Crappie	*469	*27	*100	*418	*89		
Panfish							
White bass, striped bass, striped bass hybrids	511	29	100	*451	*88		
Black bass	*606	*34	*100	*582	*96		
Catfish, bullheads	1,027	58	100	1,007	98		
Walleye, sauger							
Northern pike, pickerel, muskie, muskie hybrids							
Steelhead							
Trout							
Salmon							
Anything[1]							
Other freshwater fish							
DAYS							
Total, all types of fish	22,616	100	100	22,099	98	*518	*2
Crappie	*6,383	*28	*100	*6,044	*95		
Panfish							
White bass, striped bass, striped bass hybrids	3,318	15	100	*2,938	*89		
Black bass	*5,561	*25	*100	*5,384	*97		
Catfish, bullheads	15,958	71	100	15,791	99		
Walleye, sauger							
Northern pike, pickerel, muskie, muskie hybrids							
Steelhead							
Trout							
Salmon							
Anything[1]							
Other freshwater fish							

* Estimate based on a sample size of 10–29   ... Sample size too small (less than 10) to report data reliably

[1] Respondent fished for no specific species and identified "Anything" from a list of categories of fish

Note: Detail does not add to total because of multiple responses

Table 8. Great Lakes Anglers, Trips, and Days of Fishing in Texas: 2011

This table does not apply to this state.

Table 9. Great Lakes Anglers and Days of Fishing in Texas by Type of Fish: 2011

This table does not apply to this state.

Table 10. Saltwater Anglers, Trips, and Days of Fishing in Texas: 2011

(Population 16 years old and older. Numbers in thousands)

Anglers, trips, and days of fishing	Activity in Texas					
	Total, state residents and nonresidents		State residents		Nonresidents	
	Number	Percent	Number	Percent	Number	Percent
Total anglers	751	100	685	91	*66	*9
Total trips	5,203	100	4,882	94	*321	*6
Total days	8,157	100	7,562	93	*595	*7
Average days of fishing	11	(X)	11	(X)	*9	(X)

* Estimate based on a sample size of 10–29   (X) Not applicable

Note: Detail does not add to total because of multiple responses

Table 11. Saltwater Anglers and Days of Fishing in Texas by Type of Fish: 2011

(Population 16 years old and older. Numbers in thousands)

Anglers and days of fishing	Activity in Texas					
	Total, state residents and nonresidents			State residents		Nonresidents	
	Number	Percent of total types	Percent of anglers/days	Number	Percent of anglers/days	Number	Percent of anglers/days
ANGLERS							
Total, all types of fish	**751**	**100**	**100**	**685**	**91**	***66**	***9**
Salmon							
Striped bass							
Bluefish							
Flatfish (flounder, halibut)	*200	*27	*100	*191	*95		
Red drum (redfish)	520	69	100	505	97		
Seatrout (weakfish)	*293	*39	*100	*289	*98		
Mackerel							
Mahi Mahi (dolphinfish)							
Tuna							
Shellfish							
Anything[1]							
Another type of saltwater fish	*231	*31	*100	*219	*95		
DAYS							
Total, all types of fish	**8,157**	**100**	**100**	**7,562**	**93**	***595**	***7**
Salmon							
Striped bass							
Bluefish							
Flatfish (flounder, halibut)	*3,783	*46	*100	*3,446	*91		
Red drum (redfish)	7,090	87	100	*6,732	*95		
Seatrout (weakfish)	*4,776	*59	*100	*4,481	*94		
Mackerel							
Mahi Mahi (dolphinfish)							
Tuna							
Shellfish							
Anything[1]							
Another type of saltwater fish	*1,655	*20	*100	*1,590	*96		

* Estimate based on a sample size of 10–29   … Sample size too small (less than 10) to report data reliably

[1] Respondent fished for no specific species and identified "Anything" from a list of categories of fish

Note: Detail does not add to total because of multiple responses

Table 12. Hunters, Trips, and Days of Hunting in Texas by Type of Hunting: 2011

(Population 16 years old and older. Numbers in thousands)

Hunters, trips, and days of hunting	Activity in Texas					
	Total, state residents and nonresidents		State residents		Nonresidents	
	Number	Percent	Number	Percent	Number	Percent
HUNTERS						
Total, all hunting..........................	**1,147**	**100**	**1,080**	**94**	***67**	***6**
Big game	937	100	893	95	*43	*5
Small game	*247	*100	*243	*98		
Migratory birds	*391	*100	*379	*97		
Other animals	432	100	*398	*92	*34	*8
TRIPS						
Total, all hunting..........................	**19,956**	**100**	**19,233**	**96**	***724**	***4**
Big game	9,516	100	9,067	95	*449	*5
Small game	*3,709	*100	*3,652	*98		
Migratory birds	*1,632	*100	*1,611	*99		
Other animals	5,099	100	*4,902	*96	*197	*4
DAYS						
Total, all hunting..........................	**20,372**	**100**	**19,778**	**97**	***594**	***3**
Big game	12,651	100	12,237	97	*414	*3
Small game	*3,238	*100	*3,229	*100		
Migratory birds	*1,672	*100	*1,611	*96		
Other animals	7,882	100	*7,519	*95	*363	*5

* Estimate based on a sample size of 10–29   ... Sample size too small (less than 10) to report data reliably

Note: Detail does not add to total because of multiple responses

Table 13. Hunters and Days of Hunting in Texas by Type of Game: 2011

(Population 16 years old and older. Numbers in thousands)

Type of game	Hunters, state residents and nonresidents		Days of hunting	
	Number	Percent	Number	Percent
Total, all types of game.....................	**1,147**	**100**	**20,372**	**100**
Big game, total..........................	**937**	**82**	**12,651**	**62**
Deer	930	81	12,423	61
Elk				
Bear				
Wild turkey				
Other big game				
Small game, total......................	***247**	***22**	***3,238**	***16**
Rabbit, hare				
Quail				
Grouse/prairie chicken				
Squirrel				
Pheasant				
Other small game				
Migratory birds, total...................	***391**	***34**	***1,672**	***8**
Waterfowl				
Geese				
Ducks				
Doves	*324	*28	*1,312	*6
Other migratory birds				
Other animals, total[1].....................	**432**	**38**	**7,882**	**39**

* Estimate based on a sample size of 10–29   ... Sample size too small (less than 10) to report data reliably

[1] Includes groundhog, raccoon, fox, coyote, crow, prairie dog, etc

Note: Detail does not add to total because of multiple responses

Table 14. Hunters and Days of Hunting in Texas by Type of Land: 2011

(Population 16 years old and older. Numbers in thousands)

Hunters and days of hunting	Total, state residents and nonresidents		State residents		Nonresidents	
	Number	Percent	Number	Percent	Number	Percent
HUNTERS						
Total, all types of land......................	1,147	100	1,080	100	*67	*100
Public land, total........................	...	...	...	...	...	...
Public land only						
Public and private land						
Private land, total	1,076	94	1,013	94	*62	*93
Private land only	1,053	92	997	92	*57	*85
Private and public land						
DAYS						
Total, all types of land......................	20,372	100	19,778	100	*594	*100
Public land[1]						
Private land[2]	24,852	122	24,281	123	*570	*96

* Estimate based on a sample size of 10–29   ... Sample size too small (less than 10) to report data reliably

[1] Days of hunting on public land includes both days spent solely on public land and those spent on public and private land

[2] Days of hunting on private land includes both days spent solely on private land and those spent on private and public land

Note: Detail does not add to total because of multiple responses and nonresponse

Table 15. Selected Characteristics of Texas Resident Anglers and Hunters: 2011

(Population 16 years old and older. Numbers in thousands)

Characteristic	Population		Sportspersons (fished or hunted)			Anglers			Hunters		
	Number	Percent	Number	Percent who participated	Percent of sportspersons	Number	Percent who participated	Percent of anglers	Number	Percent who participated	Percent of hunters
Total persons	**18,681**	**100**	**2,711**	**15**	**100**	**2,355**	**13**	**100**	**1,080**	**6**	**100**
Population Density of Residence											
Urban	13,967	75	1,874	13	69	1,684	12	72	*641	*5	*59
Rural	4,714	25	837	18	31	671	14	28	*439	*9	*41
Population Size of Residence											
Metropolitan Statistical Area (MSA)	18,077	97	2,580	14	95	2,330	13	99	949	5	88
1,000,000 or more	13,036	70	1,672	13	62	1,546	12	66	*527	*4	*49
250,000 to 999,999	1,747	9	*281	*16	*10	*281	*16	*12			
50,000 to 249,999	3,294	18	626	19	23	503	15	21	*405	*12	*37
Outside MSA	604	3									
Sex											
Male	8,732	47	2,109	24	78	1,799	21	76	946	11	88
Female	9,949	53	*602	*6	*22	*556	*6	*24			
Age											
16 to 17 years	852	5									
18 to 24 years	2,084	11	*232	*11	*9	*222	*11	*9			
25 to 34 years	3,589	19	*476	*13	*18	*476	*13	*20			
35 to 44 years	2,858	15	*516	*18	*19	*481	*17	*20			
45 to 54 years	3,949	21	*454	*11	*17	*379	*10	*16	*194	*5	*18
55 to 64 years	2,869	15	*625	*22	*23	*480	*17	*20	*380	*13	*35
65 years and older	2,480	13	*321	*13	*12	*230	*9	*10			
65 to 74 years	1,943	10	*314	*16	*12	*223	*11	*9			
75 and older	537	3									
Ethnicity											
Hispanic	6,700	36	*471	*7	*17	*411	*6	*17			
Non-Hispanic	11,981	64	2,240	19	83	1,943	16	83	994	8	92
Race											
White	13,188	71	2,129	16	79	1,773	13	75	918	7	85
African American	1,879	10									
All others	3,613	19									
Annual Household Income											
Less than $20,000	3,040	16	*323	*11	*12	*245	*8	*10			
$20,000 to $29,999	1,988	11									
$30,000 to $39,999	2,003	11	*268	*13	*10						
$40,000 to $49,999	1,362	7									
$50,000 to $74,999	2,396	13	*452	*19	*17	*417	*17	*18			
$75,000 to $99,999	1,743	9	*325	*19	*12	*325	*19	*14			
$100,000 to $149,999	2,370	13	*462	*20	*17	*303	*13	*13	*264	*11	*24
$150,000 or more	1,101	6	*229	*21	*8	*229	*21	*10			
Not reported	2,678	14									
Education											
11 years or less	3,628	19	*620	*17	*23	*551	*15	*23			
12 years	5,781	31	521	9	19	468	8	20	*173	*3	*16
1 to 3 years of college	3,960	21	652	16	24	*544	*14	*23	*220	*6	*20
4 years or more of college	5,312	28	918	17	34	*792	*15	*34	*533	*10	*49

* Estimate based on a sample size of 10–29   ... Sample size too small (less than 10) to report data reliably

Note: Detail does not add to total because of multiple responses Percent who participated columns show the percent of each row's population who participated in the activity named by the column (the percent of those living in urban areas who fished, etc) Remaining percent columns show the percent of each column's participants who are described by the row heading (the percent of anglers who lived in urban areas, etc)

Table 16. Summary of Expenditures in Texas by State Residents and Nonresidents Combined for Fishing and Hunting: 2011

(Population 16 years old and older)

Expenditure item	Amount (thousands of dollars)	Spenders (thousands)	Average per spender (dollars)[1]	Average per sportsperson (dollars)[1]
FISHING AND HUNTING				
Total	**4,399,085**	**2,467**	**1,783**	**1,596**
Food and lodging	755,260	1,844	410	278
Transportation	677,236	1,991	340	244
Other trip costs[2]	450,313	1,646	274	166
Equipment (fishing, hunting)	551,863	1,809	305	191
Auxiliary equipment[3]	213,311	718	297	71
Special equipment[4]				
Magazines, books, and DVDs	*15,676	*241	*65	*6
Membership dues and contributions				
Other[5]	468,106	1,386	338	173
FISHING				
Total	**1,540,434**	**1,957**	**787**	**667**
Food and lodging	422,885	1,564	270	188
Transportation	297,817	1,682	177	126
Other trip costs[2]	324,629	1,490	218	145
Fishing equipment	203,698	1,431	142	79
Auxiliary equipment[3]	*27,174	*217	*125	*11
Special equipment[4]				
Magazines, books, and DVDs				
Membership dues and contributions				
Other[5]	17,636	539	33	8
HUNTING				
Total	**1,835,098**	**1,150**	**1,596**	**1,592**
Food and lodging	332,375	823	404	290
Transportation	379,419	900	421	331
Other trip costs[2]	*125,685	*413	*305	*110
Hunting equipment	343,969	761	452	292
Auxiliary equipment[3]	*154,067	*411	*375	*134
Special equipment[4]				
Magazines, books, and DVDs				
Membership dues and contributions				
Other[5]	450,471	887	508	393
UNSPECIFIED[6]				
Total	***925,683**	***212**	***4,371**	***341**

* Estimate based on a sample size of 10–29   ... Sample size too small (less than 10) to report data reliably

[1] Average expenditures are annual estimates

[2] Includes boating costs, equipment rental, guide fees, access fees, heating and cooking fuel, and ice and bait (for fishing only)

[3] Includes sleeping bags, packs, duffel bags, tents, binoculars and field glasses, special fishing and hunting clothing, foul weather gear, boots and waders, maintenance and repair of equipment, processing and taxidermy costs, and electronic equipment such as a GPS device

[4] Includes big-ticket items bought primarily for hunting and fishing including boats, campers, cabins, trail bikes, dune buggies, 4 x 4 vehicles, ATVs, 4-wheelers, snowmobiles, pickups, vans, travel and tent trailers, motor homes, house trailers, recreational vehicles (RVs) and other special equipment

[5] Includes land leasing and ownership, licenses, stamps, tags, permits, and plantings (for hunting only)

[6] Respondent could not specify whether expenditure was primarily for either fishing or hunting

Note: Detail does not add to total because of multiple responses and nonresponse

Table 17. Summary of Fishing Trip and Equipment Expenditures in Texas by State Residents and Nonresidents Combined by Type of Fishing: 2011

(Population 16 years old and older)

Expenditure item	Amount (thousands of dollars)	Spenders (thousands)	Average per spender (dollars)[1]	Average per angler (dollars)[1]
ALL FISHING				
Total	**1,516,520**	**1,869**	811	656
Food and lodging	422,885	1,564	270	188
Transportation	297,817	1,682	177	126
Other trip costs	324,629	1,490	218	145
Equipment	471,190	1,453	324	198
ALL FRESHWATER				
Total	**608,287**	**1,512**	402	256
Food and lodging	183,821	1,242	148	82
Transportation	183,460	1,349	136	78
Other trip costs	116,088	1,118	104	52
Equipment	124,917	1,116	112	44
FRESHWATER, EXCEPT GREAT LAKES				
Total	**608,287**	**1,512**	402	256
Food and lodging	183,821	1,242	148	82
Transportation	183,460	1,349	136	78
Other trip costs	116,088	1,118	104	52
Equipment	124,917	1,116	112	44
GREAT LAKES				
Total	...	...	...	...
Food and lodging				
Transportation				
Other trip costs				
Equipment				
SALTWATER				
Total	**890,556**	**684**	1,303	394
Food and lodging	239,063	549	435	106
Transportation	114,357	634	180	48
Other trip costs	208,540	582	358	93
Equipment	*328,596	*365	*900	*146

* Estimate based on a sample size of 10–29   ... Sample size too small (less than 10) to report data reliably

[1] Average expenditures are annual estimates

Note: Detail does not add to total because of multiple responses and nonresponse See Table 19 for detailed listing of expenditure items

Table 18. Summary of Hunting Trip and Equipment Expenditures in Texas by State Residents and Nonresidents Combined by Type of Hunting: 2011

(Population 16 years old and older)

Expenditure item	Amount (thousands of dollars)	Spenders (thousands)	Average per spender (dollars)[1]	Average per type of hunter (dollars)[1]
ALL HUNTING				
Total	**1,375,077**	**1,137**	**1,209**	**1,191**
Food and lodging	332,375	823	404	290
Transportation	379,419	900	421	331
Other trip costs	*125,685	*413	*305	*110
Equipment	537,597	814	660	461
BIG GAME				
Total	**933,460**	**897**	**1,040**	**807**
Food and lodging	209,432	613	342	183
Transportation	275,889	710	389	241
Other trip costs	*101,457	*334	*304	*88
Equipment	346,682	530	654	*295
SMALL GAME				
Total	***66,684**	***173**	***386**	***94**
Food and lodging				
Transportation				
Other trip costs				
Equipment				
MIGRATORY BIRDS				
Total	***83,250**	***371**	***225**	***133**
Food and lodging	*29,026	*337	*86	*47
Transportation	*30,691	*294	*104	*49
Other trip costs				
Equipment	*15,360	*134	*115	
OTHER ANIMALS				
Total	***134,309**	***271**	***496**	***310**
Food and lodging	*69,418	*253	*274	*161
Transportation	*55,202	*239	*231	*128
Other trip costs				
Equipment				

* Estimate based on a sample size of 10–29   ... Sample size too small (less than 10) to report data reliably

[1] Average expenditures are annual estimates

Note: Detail does not add to total because of multiple responses and nonresponse See Table 20 for detailed listing of expenditure items

Table 19. Expenditures in Texas by State Residents and Nonresidents Combined for Fishing: 2011

(Population 16 years old and older)

Expenditure item	Expenditures		Spenders		
	Amount (thousands of dollars)	Average per angler (dollars)[1]	Number (thousands)	Percent of anglers	Average per spender (dollars)[1]
Total, all items	1,540,434	667	1,957	87	787
TRIP-RELATED EXPENDITURES					
Total trip-related	1,045,330	459	1,792	80	583
Food and lodging, total	422,885	188	1,564	70	270
Food	340,678	152	1,564	70	218
Lodging	*82,207	*37	*331	*15	*248
Transportation	297,817	126	1,682	75	177
Other trip costs, total	324,629	145	1,490	66	218
Privilege and other fees[2]	65,709	29	675	30	97
Boating costs[3]	*152,410	*68	*355	*16	*429
Bait	69,023	31	1,124	50	61
Ice	34,993	16	1,050	47	33
Heating and cooking fuel					
EQUIPMENT AND OTHER EXPENDITURES PRIMARILY FOR FISHING					
Fishing equipment, total	203,698	79	1,431	64	142
Reels, rods, and rod-making components	84,274	*26	547	24	154
Lines, hooks, sinkers, etc	60,015	27	1,030	46	58
Artificial lures and flies	36,656	16	857	38	43
Creels, stringers, fish bags, landing nets, and gaff hooks					
Minnow seines, traps, and bait containers	*4,268	*2	*125	*6	*34
Other fishing equipment[4]	*14,218	*6	*357	*16	*40
Auxiliary equipment[5]	*27,174	*11	*217	*10	*125
Special equipment[6]					
Other fishing costs[7]	23,914	11	628	28	38

* Estimate based on a sample size of 10–29   ... Sample size too small (less than 10) to report data reliably

[1] Average expenditures are annual estimates

[2] Includes boat or equipment rental and fees for guides, pack trip (party and charter boats, etc), public land use, and private land use

[3] Includes boat launching, mooring, storage, maintenance, insurance, pumpout fees, and fuel

[4] Includes electronic fishing devices (depth finders, fish finders, etc), tackle boxes, ice fishing equipment, and other fishing equipment

[5] Includes sleeping bags, packs, duffel bags, tents, binoculars and field glasses, special fishing clothing, foul weather gear, boots and waders, maintenance and repair of equipment, processing and taxidermy costs, and electronic equipment such as a GPS device

[6] Includes big-ticket items bought primarily for fishing including boats, campers, cabins, trail bikes, dune buggies, 4 x 4 vehicles, ATVs, 4-wheelers, snowmobiles, pickups, vans, travel and tent trailers, motor homes, house trailers, recreational vehicles (RVs) and other special equipment

[7] Includes magazines, books, and DVDs, membership dues and contributions, land leasing and ownership, and licenses, stamps, tags, and permits

Note: Detail does not add to total because of multiple responses and nonresponse   Percent of anglers may be greater than 100 because spenders who did not fish in this state are included

Table 20. Expenditures in Texas by State Residents and Nonresidents Combined for Hunting: 2011

(Population 16 years old and older)

Expenditure item	Expenditures		Spenders		
	Amount (thousands of dollars)	Average per hunter (dollars)[1]	Number (thousands)	Percent of hunters	Average per spender (dollars)[1]
Total, all items	1,835,098	1,592	1,150	100	1,596
TRIP-RELATED EXPENDITURES					
Total trip-related	837,479	730	940	82	891
Food and lodging, total	332,375	290	823	72	404
Food	290,002	253	823	72	352
Lodging	*42,374	*37	*112	*10	*378
Transportation	379,419	331	900	79	421
Other trip costs, total	*125,685	*110	*413	*36	*305
Privilege and other fees[2]	*109,848	*96	*118	*10	*930
Boating costs[3]					
Heating and cooking fuel	*15,837	*14	*339	*30	*47
EQUIPMENT AND OTHER EXPENDITURES PRIMARILY FOR HUNTING					
Hunting equipment, total	343,969	292	761	66	452
Firearms	*142,534		*194	*17	*735
Ammunition	73,722	63	675	59	109
Other hunting equipment[4]	*127,713	*107	*465	*41	*275
Auxiliary equipment[5]	*154,067	*134	*411	*36	*375
Special equipment[6]					
Other hunting costs[7]	460,022	401	898	78	512

* Estimate based on a sample size of 10–29   ... Sample size too small (less than 10) to report data reliably

[1] Average expenditures are annual estimates

[2] Includes guide fees, pack trip and package fees, public and private land use access fees, and rental of equipment such as boats and hunting or camping equipment

[3] Boating costs include launching, mooring, storage, maintenance, insurance, pumpout fees, and fuel

[4] Includes telescopic sights, decoys and game calls, handloading equipment and components, hunting dogs and associated costs, hunting knives, bows, arrows, archery equipment, and other hunting equipment

[5] Includes sleeping bags, packs, duffel bags, tents, binoculars and field glasses, special hunting clothing, foul weather gear, boots and waders, maintenance and repair of equipment, processing and taxidermy costs, and electronic equipment such as a GPS device

[6] Includes big-ticket items bought primarily for hunting including boats, campers, cabins, trail bikes, dune buggies, 4 x 4 vehicles, ATVs, 4-wheelers, snowmobiles, pickups, vans, travel and tent trailers, motor homes, house trailers, recreational vehicles (RVs) and other special equipment

[7] Includes magazines, books, and DVDs, membership dues and contributions, land leasing and ownership, and licenses, stamps, tags, and permits

Note: Detail does not add to total because of multiple responses and nonresponse Percent of hunters may be greater than 100 because spenders who did not hunt in this state are included

Table 21. Trip and Equipment Expenditures in Texas for Fishing and Hunting by Texas Residents and Nonresidents: 2011

(Population 16 years old and older)

Expenditure item	Amount (thousands of dollars)	Spenders (thousands)	Average per spender (dollars)[1]	Average per sportsperson (dollars)[1]
STATE RESIDENTS AND NONRESIDENTS				
Trip and equipment expenditures for fishing and hunting, total	**3,830,785**	**2,366**	**1,619**	**3,341**
Trip and equipment expenditures for fishing, total	**1,518,543**	**1,955**	**777**	**656**
Food and lodging	422,885	1,564	270	188
Transportation	297,817	1,682	177	126
Boating costs[2]	*152,410	*355	*429	*68
Other trip costs[3]	172,218	1,482	116	77
Equipment	473,213	1,539	307	198
Trip and equipment expenditures for hunting, total	**1,395,641**	**1,177**	**1,186**	**1,191**
Food and lodging	332,375	823	404	290
Transportation	379,419	900	421	331
Boating costs[2]				
Other trip costs[3]	*125,685	*413	*305	*110
Equipment	558,162	854	654	461
Unspecified equipment[4]	...	...	...	...
STATE RESIDENTS				
Trip and equipment expenditures for fishing and hunting, total	**3,552,540**	**2,103**	**1,689**	**3,290**
Trip and equipment expenditures for fishing, total	**1,395,894**	**1,801**	**775**	**647**
Food and lodging	394,203	1,499	263	185
Transportation	279,214	1,619	172	124
Boating costs[2]	*132,662	*314	*423	*62
Other trip costs[3]	156,701	1,412	111	73
Equipment	433,113	1,409	307	202
Trip and equipment expenditures for hunting, total	**1,240,046**	**1,061**	**1,168**	**1,145**
Food and lodging	271,767	765	355	252
Transportation	352,236	842	418	326
Boating costs[2]				
Other trip costs[3]	*87,638	*371	*236	*81
Equipment	528,404	777	680	486
Unspecified equipment[4]	...	...	...	...
NONRESIDENTS				
Trip and equipment expenditures for fishing and hunting, total	**278,245**	**263**	**1,056**	**4,166**
Trip and equipment expenditures for fishing, total	***122,649**	***154**	***795**	***839**
Food and lodging	*28,681	*65	*439	*252
Transportation	*18,603	*63	*294	*164
Boating costs[2]				
Other trip costs[3]	*15,517	*70	*223	*136
Equipment	*40,100	*130	*308	
Trip and equipment expenditures for hunting, total	**155,596**	**115**	**1,348**	***1,939**
Food and lodging	*60,608	*58	*1,046	*907
Transportation	*27,182	*59	*465	*407
Boating costs[2]				
Other trip costs[3]	*38,047	*41	*920	*570
Equipment	*29,758	*76	*390	
Unspecified equipment[4]	...	...	...	...

* Estimate based on a sample size of 10–29   ... Sample size too small (less than 10) to report data reliably

[1] Average expenditures are annual estimates

[2] Includes boat launching, mooring, storage, maintenance, insurance, pumpout fees, and fuel

[3] Includes equipment rental, guide and access fees, ice and bait for fishing, and heating and cooking oil

[4] Respondent could not specify whether item was for hunting or fishing

Note: Detail does not add to total because of multiple responses and nonresponse

Table 22. Summary of Texas Residents' Fishing and Hunting Expenditures Both Inside and Outside Texas: 2011

(Population 16 years old and older)

Expenditure item	Amount (thousands of dollars)	Spenders (thousands)	Average per spender (dollars)[1]	Average per sportsperson (dollars)[1]
FISHING AND HUNTING				
Total	**4,420,858**	**2,435**	**1,815**	**1,631**
Food and lodging	777,071	1,875	415	287
Transportation	733,016	2,089	351	270
Other trip costs[2]	431,161	1,655	261	159
Equipment (fishing, hunting)	546,955	1,679	326	202
Auxiliary equipment[3]	195,751	672	291	72
Special equipment[4]				
Magazines, books, and DVDs	*22,196	*243	*92	*8
Membership dues and contributions				
Other[5]	447,348	1,483	302	165
FISHING				
Total	**1,711,265**	**2,079**	**823**	**727**
Food and lodging	488,598	1,672	292	208
Transportation	378,176	1,870	202	161
Other trip costs[2]	351,187	1,562	225	149
Fishing equipment	193,256	1,368	141	82
Auxiliary equipment[3]	*27,589	*192	*144	*12
Special equipment[4]				
Magazines, books, and DVDs				
Membership dues and contributions				
Other[5]	25,764	769	34	11
HUNTING				
Total	**1,696,128**	**1,036**	**1,638**	**1,571**
Food and lodging	288,473	765	377	267
Transportation	354,840	842	422	329
Other trip costs[2]	*79,973	*371	*215	*74
Hunting equipment	349,720	729	480	324
Auxiliary equipment[3]	*152,824	*401	*381	*142
Special equipment[4]				
Magazines, books, and DVDs				
Membership dues and contributions				
Other[5]	421,584	865	487	390
UNSPECIFIED[6]				
Total	*1,007,826	*219	*4,608	*372

* Estimate based on a sample size of 10–29   ... Sample size too small (less than 10) to report data reliably

[1] Average expenditures are annual estimates

[2] Includes boating costs, equipment rental, guide fees, access fees, heating and cooking fuel, and ice and bait (for fishing only)

[3] Includes sleeping bags, packs, duffel bags, tents, binoculars and field glasses, special fishing and hunting clothing, foul weather gear, boots and waders, maintenance and repair of equipment, processing and taxidermy costs, and electronic equipment such as a GPS device

[4] Includes big-ticket items bought primarily for hunting and fishing including boats, campers, cabins, trail bikes, dune buggies, 4 x 4 vehicles, ATVs, 4-wheelers, snowmobiles, pickups, vans, travel and tent trailers, motor homes, house trailers, recreational vehicles (RVs) and other special equipment

[5] Includes land leasing and ownership, licenses, stamps, tags, and permits, and plantings (for hunting only)

[6] Respondent could not specify whether expenditure was primarily for fishing or hunting

Note: Detail does not add to total because of multiple responses and nonresponse See Tables 19–20 for a detailed listing of expenditure items

Table 23. In-State and Out-of-State Expenditures by Texas Residents for Fishing and Hunting: 2011

(State population 16 years old and older)

Expenditure item	Amount (thousands of dollars)	Spenders (thousands)	Average per spender (dollars)[1]	Average per sportsperson (dollars)[1]
IN TEXAS				
Expenditures for fishing and hunting, total	**4,088,942**	**2,190**	**1,867**	**1,507**
Trip-related expenditures	1,674,423	1,959	855	617
Equipment (fishing and hunting)	505,214	1,616	313	186
Auxiliary equipment[2]	190,102	665	286	70
Special equipment[3]				
Other[4]	536,403	1,378	389	198
Expenditures for fishing, total	**1,417,257**	**1,793**	**790**	**631**
Trip-related expenditures	962,781	1,716	561	429
Fishing equipment	169,049	1,302	130	75
Auxiliary equipment[2]				
Special equipment[3]				
Other[4]	23,169	593	39	10
Expenditures for hunting, total	**1,665,082**	**1,036**	**1,608**	**1,452**
Trip-related expenditures	711,642	878	811	621
Hunting equipment	332,186	698	476	290
Auxiliary equipment[2]	*152,824	*401	*381	*133
Special equipment[3]				
Other[4]	428,869	874	491	374
Unspecified expenditures for fishing and hunting, total[5]	***1,000,964**	***212**	***4,726**	***369**
OUT OF STATE				
Expenditures for fishing and hunting, total	***470,477**	***2,006**	***235**	***173**
Trip-related expenditures	*405,386	*546	*742	*149
Equipment (fishing and hunting)				
Auxiliary equipment[2]				
Special equipment[3]				
Other[4]	*17,701	*737	*24	*7
Expenditures for fishing, total	***376,979**	***1,690**	***223**	***168**
Trip-related expenditures	*338,151	*515	*656	*151
Fishing equipment				
Auxiliary equipment[2]				
Special equipment[3]				
Other[4]	*8,972	*388	*23	*4
Expenditures for hunting, total	...	...	...	...
Trip-related expenditures				
Hunting equipment				
Auxiliary equipment[2]				
Special equipment[3]				
Other[4]				
Unspecified expenditures for fishing and hunting, total[5]	...	...	...	...

* Estimate based on a sample size of 10–29   ... Sample size too small (less than 10) to report data reliably

[1] Average expenditures are annual estimates

[2] Auxiliary equipment includes sleeping bags, packs, duffel bags, tents, binoculars and field glasses, special fishing and hunting clothing, foul weather gear, boots and waders, maintenance and repair of equipment, processing and taxidermy costs, and electronic equipment such as a GPS device

[3] Special equipment includes boats, campers, cabins, trail bikes, dune buggies, 4 x 4 vehicles, ATVs, 4-wheelers, snowmobiles, pickups, vans, travel and tent trailers, motor homes, house trailers, recreational vehicles (RVs) and other special equipment

[4] Other equipment includes expenditures for magazines, books, DVDs, membership dues and contributions, land leasing and ownership, licenses, stamps, tags, and permits, and plantings

[5] Respondent could not specify whether expenditure was primarily for either fishing or hunting

Note: Detail does not add to total because of multiple responses and nonresponse

Table 24. Wildlife Watching in Texas by State Residents and Nonresidents Combined: 2011

(Population 16 years old and older. Numbers in thousands)

Participants	Number	Percent
Total participants	**4,376**	**100**
Away from home	1,026	23
Observe wildlife	1,024	23
Photograph wildlife	*519	*12
Feed wildlife	*651	*15
Around the home	4,249	97
Observe wildlife	3,197	73
Photograph wildlife	1,529	35
Feed wildlife	3,401	78
Visit parks or natural areas[1]	*428	*10
Maintain plantings or natural areas	*780	*18

* Estimate based on a sample size of 10–29

[1] Includes visits only to parks or natural areas within one mile of home

Note: Detail does not add to total because of multiple responses

Table 25. Participants, Trips, and Days of Participation in Away-From-Home Wildlife Watching in Texas: 2011

(Population 16 years old and older. Numbers in thousands)

Participants, trips, and days of participation	Activity in Texas					
	Total, state residents and nonresidents		State residents		Nonresidents	
	Number	Percent	Number	Percent	Number	Percent
PARTICIPANTS						
Total participants	**1,026**	**100**	***899**	***100**	***127**	***100**
Observe wildlife	1,024	100	*899	*100	*125	*98
Photograph wildlife	*519	*51	*410	*46	*109	*86
Feed wildlife	*651	*63	*630	*70		
TRIPS						
Total Trips	**12,401**	**100**	***12,097**	***100**	***304**	***100**
Average days per trip	1	(X)	*1	(X)	*5	(X)
DAYS						
Total days..................................	**11,840**	**100**	***10,441**	***100**	***1,399**	***100**
Observing wildlife	9,780	83	*8,590	*82	*1,190	*85
Photographing wildlife	*3,831	*32			*1,093	*78
Feeding wildlife	*8,014	*68	*7,340	*70		
Average days per participant.....................	**12**	**(X)**	***12**	**(X)**	***11**	**(X)**
Observing wildlife	10	(X)	*10	(X)	*10	(X)
Photographing wildlife	*7	(X)		(X)	*10	(X)
Feeding wildlife	*12	(X)	*12	(X)		(X)

* Estimate based on a sample size of 10–29   ... Sample size too small (less than 10) to report data reliably   (X) Not applicable

Note: Detail does not add to total because of multiple responses and nonresponse

Table 26. Away-From-Home Wildlife-Watching Participants by Wildlife Observed, Photographed, or Fed in Texas: 2011

(Population 16 years old and older. Numbers in thousands)

Wildlife observed, photographed, or fed	Total, state residents and nonresidents		State residents		Nonresidents	
	Number	Percent	Number	Percent	Number	Percent
Total all wildlife................................	**1,026**	**100**	***899**	***88**	***127**	***12**
Total birds.......................................	**882**	**100**	***756**	***86**	***125**	***14**
Songbirds (cardinals, robins, warblers, etc)	*647	*100	*590	*91	*57	*9
Birds of prey (hawks, owls, eagles, etc)	*399	*100	*350	*88	*49	*12
Waterfowl (ducks, geese, swans, etc)	*492	*100	*390	*79	*102	*21
Other water birds (shorebirds, herons, cranes, etc)	*482	*100	*382	*79	*100	*21
Other birds (pheasants, turkeys, road runners, etc)	*296	*100				
Total land mammals.............................	***824**	***100**	***722**	***88**	...	...
Large land mammals (bears, bison, elk, etc)	*366	*100	*334	*91		
Small land mammals (prairie dogs, squirrels, etc)	*615	*100	*514	*84		
Fish (salmon, sharks, etc)	*511	*100				
Marine mammals (whales, dolphins, etc)						
Other wildlife (butterflies, turtles, etc)	*691	*100	*586	*85		

* Estimate based on a sample size of 10–29   ... Sample size too small (less than 10) to report data reliably

Note: Detail does not add to total because of multiple responses

Table 27. Participation in Wildlife-Watching Activities Around the Home in Texas: 2011

(State population 16 years old and older. Numbers in thousands)

Around the home	Participants	
	Number	Percent
Total around-the-home participants..................................	**4,249**	**100**
Observe wildlife	3,197	75
Visit parks and natural areas[1]	*428	*10
Photograph wildlife	1,529	36
Feed wildlife	3,401	80
Maintain natural areas	*493	*12
Maintain plantings	*692	*16
Participants Observing Wildlife		
Total, all wildlife	**3,197**	**100**
Birds	2,036	64
Land mammals	2,832	89
Large mammals	*1,541	*48
Small mammals	1,797	56
Amphibians or reptiles	1,233	39
Insects or spiders	*973	*30
Fish and other wildlife		
Total, 1 day or more	**3,197**	**100**
1 to 10 days	*350	*11
11 to 50 days	*463	*14
51 to 200 days	*947	*30
201 days or more	*1,438	*45
Participants Visiting Parks or Natural Areas[1]		
Total, 1 day or more	***428**	***100**
1 to 5 days		
6 to 10 days		
11 days or more		
Participants Photographing Wildlife		
Total, 1 day or more	**1,529**	**100**
1 to 3 days	*392	*26
4 to 10 days	*771	*50
11 or more days	*366	*24
Participants Feeding Wildlife		
Total, all wildlife	**3,401**	**100**
Wild birds	3,258	96
Other wildlife	*681	*20

* Estimate based on a sample size of 10–29   ... Sample size too small (less than 10) to report data reliably

[1] Includes visits only to parks or natural areas within one mile of home

Note: Detail does not add to total because of multiple responses and nonresponse

Table 28. Texas Residents Participating in Wildlife Watching in the United States: 2011

(State population 16 years old and older Numbers in thousands)

Participants	Number	Percent of participants	Percent of population
Total participants	4,263	100	23
Away from home	*977	*23	*5
Around the home	4,249	100	23
Observe wildlife	3,197	75	17
Photograph wildlife	1,529	36	8
Feed wild birds or other wildlife	3,401	80	18
Maintain plantings or natural areas	*780	*18	*4
Visit parks or natural areas[1]	*428	*10	*2

* Estimate based on a sample size of 10–29

[1] Includes visits only to parks or natural areas within one mile of home

Note: Detail does not add to total because of multiple responses The column showing percent of participants is based on total participants The column
     showing percent of population is based on the state population 16 years old and older, including those who did not participate in wildlife watching

Table 29. Wild Bird Observers and Days of Observation in Texas by State Residents and Nonresidents: 2011

(Population 16 years old and older. Numbers in thousands)

Observers and days of observation	Total, state residents and nonresidents		State residents		Nonresidents	
	Number	Percent	Number	Percent	Number	Percent
OBSERVERS						
Total bird observers	2,238	100	2,115	100	*123	*100
Around-the-home observers	2,036	91	2,036	96	(X)	(X)
Away-from-home observers	879	39	*756	*36	*123	*100
DAYS						
Total days observing birds	295,257	100	294,087	100	*1,170	*100
Around the home	286,150	97	286,150	97	(X)	(X)
Away from home	9,107	3	*7,938	*3	*1,170	*100

* Estimate based on a sample size of 10–29   (X) Not applicable

Note: Detail does not add to total because of multiple responses

Table 30. Selected Characteristics of Texas Residents Participating in Wildlife Watching: 2011

(State population 16 years old and older. Numbers in thousands)

Characteristic	Population		Participants — Total			Participants — Away from home			Participants — Around the home		
	Number	Percent	Number	Percent who par-ticipated	Percent	Number	Percent who par-ticipated	Percent	Number	Percent who par-ticipated	Percent
Total persons	18,681	100	4,263	23	100	*977	*5	*100	4,249	23	100
Population Density of Residence											
Urban	13,967	75	2,081	15	49	*422	*3	*43	2,081	15	49
Rural	4,714	25	2,182	46	51	*555	*12	*57	2,168	46	51
Population Size of Residence											
Metropolitan Statistical Area (MSA)	18,077	97	4,050	22	95	*899	*5	*92	4,036	22	95
1,000,000 or more	13,036	70	3,014	23	71	*605	*5	*62	3,014	23	71
250,000 to 999,999	1,747	9	*389	*22	*9				*389	*22	*9
50,000 to 249,999	3,294	18	*647	*20	*15				*633	*19	*15
Outside MSA	604	3									
Sex											
Male	8,732	47	1,606	18	38	*389	*4	*40	1,592	18	37
Female	9,949	53	2,657	27	62	*588	*6	*60	2,657	27	63
Age											
16 to 17 years	852	5									
18 to 24 years	2,084	11									
25 to 34 years	3,589	19	*434	*12	*10				*420	*12	*10
35 to 44 years	2,858	15	*286	*10	*7				*286	*10	*7
45 to 54 years	3,949	21	*1,248	*32	*29				*1,248	*32	*29
55 to 64 years	2,869	15	*419	*15	*10				*419	*15	*10
65 years and older	2,480	13	1,726	70	40				1,726	70	41
65 to 74 years	1,943	10	*1,632	*84	*38				*1,632	*84	*38
75 and older	537	3									
Ethnicity											
Hispanic	6,700	36	*363	*5	*9				*363	*5	*9
Non-Hispanic	11,981	64	3,900	33	91	*927	*8	*95	3,886	32	91
Race											
White	13,188	71	4,029	31	95	*939	*7	*96	4,015	30	95
African American	1,879	10									
All others	3,613	19									
Annual Household Income											
Less than $20,000	3,040	16									
$20,000 to $29,999	1,988	11	*328	*16	*8						
$30,000 to $39,999	2,003	11									
$40,000 to $49,999	1,362	7	*295	*22	*7				*295	*22	*7
$50,000 to $74,999	2,396	13	*1,021	*43	*24				*1,021	*43	*24
$75,000 to $99,999	1,743	9	*349	*20	*8				*349	*20	*8
$100,000 to $149,999	2,370	13	*639	*27	*15				*639	*27	*15
$150,000 or more	1,101	6									
Not reported	2,678	14									
Education											
11 years or less	3,628	19									
12 years	5,781	31	*1,490	*26	*35				*1,490	*26	*35
1 to 3 years of college	3,960	21	*583	*15	*14				*569	*14	*13
4 years or more of college	5,312	28	1,850	35	43	*586	*11	*60	1,850	35	44

* Estimate based on a sample size of 10–29   ... Sample size too small (less than 10) to report data reliably

Note: Detail does not add to total because of multiple responses and nonresponse Percent who participated columns show the percent of each row's population who participated in the activity named by the column (the percent of those living in urban areas who participated, etc) Percent columns show the percent of each column's participants who are described by the row heading (the percent of those who participated who live in urban areas, etc)

Table 31. Expenditures in Texas by State Residents and Nonresidents Combined for Wildlife Watching: 2011

(Population 16 years old and older)

Expenditure item	Expenditures (thousands of dollars)	Average per participant (dollars)[1]	Spenders		
			Number (thousands)	Percent of wildlife-watching participants[2]	Average per spender (dollars)[1]
Total, all items...	1,823,758	413	3,658	84	499
TRIP EXPENDITURES					
Total, trip-related	478,080	463	977	95	489
Food and lodging	253,565	247	755	74	336
Food	112,865	110	723	70	156
Lodging	*140,701	*137	*421	*41	*334
Transportation	196,653	189	970	95	203
Other trip costs[3]	*27,862	*27	*310	*30	*90
EQUIPMENT AND OTHER EXPENDITURES					
Total	1,345,678	304	3,495	80	385
Wildlife-watching equipment, total...............................	590,272	132	3,319	76	178
Binoculars, spotting scopes					
Film and photo processing	*23,945	*5	*332	*8	*72
Cameras, special lenses, video cameras, and other photographic equipment, including memory cards	*37,605	*8	*275	*6	*137
Day packs, carrying cases, and special clothing	*20,442	*5	*266	*6	*77
Bird food	220,415	50	2,756	63	80
Food for other wildlife	*196,643	*44	*1,604	*37	*123
Nest boxes, bird houses, bird feeders, and bird baths	65,037	15	1,255	29	52
Other equipment (including field guides)					
Auxiliary equipment[4]	*25,487		*200	*5	*128
Special equipment[5]					
Magazines, books, and DVDs	*15,375	*3	*465	*11	*33
Membership dues and contributions	*29,245	*7	*540	*12	*54
Land leasing and ownership					
Plantings	*215,172	*49	*681	*16	*316

* Estimate based on a sample size of 10–29   ... Sample size too small (less than 10) to report data reliably

[1] Average expenditures are annual estimates

[2] Percent of wildlife-watching participants column for trip-related expenditures is based on away-from-home participation For equipment and other expenditures, the percent of wildlife-watching participants column is based on total wildlife-watching participants

[3] Includes equipment rental and fees for guides, pack trips, public land use and private land use, boat fuel, other boating costs, and heating and cooking fuel

[4] Includes tents, tarps, frame packs and other backpacking equipment, other camping equipment, and other auxiliary equipment

[5] Includes boats, campers, cabins, trail bikes, dune buggies, 4 x 4 vehicles, ATVs, 4-wheelers, snowmobiles, pickups, vans, travel and tent trailers, motor homes, house trailers, recreational vehicles (RVs) and other special equipment

Note: Detail does not add to total because of multiple responses and nonresponse

Table 32.   Trip and Equipment Expenditures in Texas for Wildlife Watching by Texas Residents and Nonresidents: 2011

(Population 16 years old and older)

Expenditure item	Amount (thousands of dollars)	Spenders (thousands)	Average per spender (dollars)[1]	Average per participant (dollars)[1]
STATE RESIDENTS AND NONRESIDENTS				
Total	**1,398,050**	**3,580**	**391**	**316**
Food and lodging	253,565	755	336	247
Transportation	196,653	970	203	189
Other trip costs[2]	*27,862	*310	*90	*27
Equipment[3]	919,971	3,321	277	207
STATE RESIDENTS				
Total	**1,178,565**	**3,376**	**349**	**277**
Food and lodging	*141,049	*635	*222	*157
Transportation	*125,490	*855	*147	*136
Other trip costs[2]				
Equipment[3]	900,082	3,217	280	212
NONRESIDENTS				
Total	***219,485**	***204**	***1,076**	***1,613**
Food and lodging	*112,517	*120	*939	*883
Transportation	*71,162	*116	*616	*559
Other trip costs[2]	*15,918	*112	*142	*125
Equipment[3]	*19,888	*104	*191	

* Estimate based on a sample size of 10–29   ... Sample size too small (less than 10) to report data reliably

[1] Average expenditures are annual estimates

[2] Includes equipment rental and fees for guides, pack trips, public land use, private land use, boat fuel, other boating costs, and heating and cooking fuel

[3] Includes wildlife-watching auxiliary and special equipment

Note: Detail does not add to total because of multiple responses and nonresponse See Table 33 for detailed listed of expenditure items

Table 33. Wildlife-Watching Expenditures Both Inside and Outside Texas by Texas Residents: 2011

(State population 16 years old and older)

Expenditure item	Expenditures (thousands of dollars)	Average per participant (dollars)[1]	Spenders		
			Number (thousands)	Percent of wildlife-watching participants[2]	Average per spender (dollars)[1]
Total, all items...	**1,677,780**	**394**	**3,455**	**81**	**486**
TRIP EXPENDITURES					
Total, trip-related	*335,013	*343	*879	*90	*381
Food and lodging	*175,550	*180	*660	*67	*266
Food	*88,731	*91	*627	*64	*141
Lodging					
Transportation	*145,769	*149	*879	*90	*166
Other trip costs[3]	*13,694	*14	*258	*26	*53
EQUIPMENT AND OTHER EXPENDITURES					
Total	**1,342,767**	**315**	**3,377**	**79**	**398**
Wildlife-watching equipment, total.......................	**587,004**	**138**	**3,217**	**75**	**182**
Binoculars, spotting scopes					
Film and photo processing	*25,343	*6	*346	*8	*73
Cameras, special lenses, video cameras, and other photographic equipment, including memory cards	*43,957	*10	*293	*7	*150
Day packs, carrying cases, and special clothing					
Bird food	220,276	52	2,740	64	80
Food for other wildlife	*193,270	*45	*1,576	*37	*123
Nest boxes, bird houses, bird feeders, and bird baths	65,646	15	1,266	30	52
Other equipment					
Auxiliary equipment[4]					
Special equipment[5]					
Magazines, books, and DVDs	*17,422	*4	*492	*12	*35
Membership dues and contributions	*32,048	*8	*537	*13	*60
Land leasing and ownership					
Plantings	*215,172	*50	*681	*16	*316

* Estimate based on a sample size of 10–29   ... Sample size too small (less than 10) to report data reliably

[1] Average expenditures are annual estimates

[2] Percent of wildlife-watching participants column for trip-related expenditures is based on away-from-home participation For equipment and other expenditures, the percent of wildlife-watching participants column is based on total wildlife-watching participants

[3] Includes equipment rental and fees for guides, pack trips, public land use and private land use, boat fuel, other boating costs, and heating and cooking fuel

[4] Includes tents, tarps, frame packs and other backpacking equipment, other camping equipment, and other auxiliary equipment

[5] Includes boats, campers, cabins, trail bikes, dune buggies, 4 x 4 vehicles, ATVs, 4-wheelers, snowmobiles, pickups, vans, travel and tent trailers, motor homes, house trailers, recreational vehicles (RVs) and other special equipment

Note: Detail does not add to total because of multiple responses and nonresponse

Table 34. In-State and Out-of-State Expenditures by Texas Residents for Wildlife Watching: 2011

(State population 16 years old and older)

Expenditure Item	Amount (thousands of dollars)	Spenders (thousands)	Average per spender (dollars)[1]	Average per participant (dollars)[1]
IN TEXAS				
Expenditures for wildlife watching, total[2]..................	**1,603,408**	**3,404**	**471**	**377**
Trip-related expenditures[3]	*278,483	*855	*326	*310
Wildlife-watching equipment[4]	574,395	3,217	179	135
Auxiliary equipment[5]				
Special equipment[6]				
Other[7]	424,843	1,207	352	100
OUT OF STATE				
Expenditures for wildlife watching, total[2]..................	...	...	...	...
Trip-related expenditures[3]				
Wildlife-watching equipment[4]				
Auxiliary equipment[5]				
Special equipment[6]				
Other[7]				

* Estimate based on a sample size of 10–29   ... Sample size too small (less than 10) to report data reliably

[1] Average expenditures are annual estimates

[2] Information on trip-related expenditures was collected for away-from-home participants only Equipment and other expenditures are based on information collected from both away-from-home and around-the-home participants

[3] Includes equipment rental and fees for guides, pack trips, public land use and private land use, boat fuel, other boating costs, and heating and cooking fuel

[4] Includes binoculars, spotting scopes, cameras, special lenses, videocameras, other photography equipment, memory cards, film and photo processing, commercially prepared and packaged wild bird food, other bulk food used to feed wild birds, food used to feed other wildlife, nest boxes, bird houses, feeders, baths, and other wildife-watching equipment

[5] Includes tents, tarps, frame packs and other backpacking equipment, other camping equipment, and other auxiliary equipment

[6] Includes boats, campers, cabins, trail bikes, dune buggies, 4 x 4 vehicles, ATVs, 4-wheelers, snowmobiles, pickups, vans, travel and tent trailers, motor homes, house trailers, recreational vehicles (RVs) and other special equipment

[7] Includes magazines, books, DVDs, membership dues and contributions, and land leasing and ownership

Note: Detail does not add to total because of multiple responses and nonresponse

Table 35. Participation of Texas Resident Wildlife-Watching Participants in Fishing and Hunting: 2011

(State population 16 years old and older. Numbers in thousands)

Participants	Total wildlife watchers		Wildife-watching activity			
			Away from home		Around the home	
	Number	Percent	Number	Percent	Number	Percent
Total participants	**4,263**	**100**	***977**	***100**	**4,249**	**100**
Wildlife-watching participants who:						
Did not fish or hunt	3,177	75	*373	*38	3,340	79
Fished or hunted	1,086	25	*605	*62	909	21
Fished	851	20	*480	*49	675	16
Hunted	*600	*14	*381	*39	*450	*11

* Estimate based on a sample size of 10–29

Note: Detail does not add to total because of multiple responses and nonresponse

Table 36. Participation of Texas Resident Sportspersons in Wildlife-Watching Activities: 2011

(State population 16 years old and older. Numbers in thousands)

Sportspersons	Sportspersons		Anglers		Hunters	
	Number	Percent	Number	Percent	Number	Percent
Total sportspersons...	2,711	100	2,355	100	1,080	100
Sportspersons who:						
Did not engage in wildlife-watching activities	1,625	60	1,503	64	480	44
Engaged in wildlife-watching activities	1,086	40	851	36	*600	*56
Away from home	*605	*22	*480	*20	*381	*35
Around the home	909	34	675	29	*450	*42

* Estimate based on a sample size of 10–29

Note: Detail does not add to total because of multiple responses and nonresponse

State reports for previous Surveys included tables that had estimates for all fifty states. In order to expedite release of the 2011 Texas State report, state estimates have been deleted. To find state estimates other than Texas, go to *http://wsfrprograms.fws.gov/Subpages/NationalSurvey/reports2011.html*. State reports are being released alphabetically, beginning in early 2013.

Appendix A

Appendix A. Definitions

Annual household income—Total 2011 income of household members before taxes and other deductions.

Around-the-home wildlife watching—Activity within 1 mile of home with one of six primary purposes: (1) taking special interest in or trying to identify birds or other wildlife; (2) photographing wildlife; (3) feeding birds or other wildlife; (4) maintaining natural areas of at least one-quarter acre for the benefit of wildlife; (5) maintaining plantings (such as shrubs and agricultural crops) for the benefit of wildlife; and (6) visiting parks and natural areas to observe, photograph, or feed wildlife.

Auxiliary equipment—Equipment owned primarily for wildlife-associated recreation. For the sportspersons section, these include sleeping bags, packs, duffel bags, tents, binoculars and field glasses, special fishing and hunting clothing, foul weather gear, boots and waders, maintenance and repair of equipment, and processing and taxidermy costs. For the wildlife-watching section, these include tents, tarps, frame packs, backpacking and other camping equipment, and blinds. For both sportspersons and wildlife watchers, it also includes electronic auxiliary equipment such as Global Positioning Systems.

Away-from-home wildlife watching—Trips or outings at least 1 mile from home for the primary purpose of observing, photographing, or feeding wildlife. Trips to zoos, circuses, aquariums, and museums are not included.

Big game—Bear, deer, elk, moose, wild turkey, and similar large animals that are hunted.

Census Divisions

East North Central
Illinois
Indiana
Michigan
Ohio
Wisconsin

East South Central
Alabama
Kentucky
Mississippi
Tennessee

Middle Atlantic
New Jersey
New York
Pennsylvania

Mountain
Arizona
Colorado
Idaho
Montana
Nevada
New Mexico
Utah
Wyoming

New England
Connecticut
Maine
Massachusetts
New Hampshire
Rhode Island
Vermont

Pacific
Alaska
California
Hawaii
Oregon
Washington

South Atlantic
Delaware
District of Columbia
Florida
Georgia
Maryland
North Carolina
South Carolina
Virginia
West Virginia

West North Central
Kansas
Iowa
Minnesota
Missouri
Nebraska
North Dakota
South Dakota

West South Central
Arkansas
Louisiana
Oklahoma
Texas

Day—Any part of a day spent participating in a given activity. For example, if someone hunted two hours one day and three hours another day, it would be reported as two days of hunting. If someone hunted two hours in the morning and three hours in the afternoon of the same day, it would be considered one day of hunting.

Education—The highest completed grade of school or year of college.

Expenditures—Money spent in 2011 for wildlife-related recreation trips in the United States, wildlife-related recreational equipment purchased in the United States, and other items. The "other items" were books, magazines, and DVDs; membership dues and contributions, land leasing or owning; hunting and fishing licenses; and plantings, all for the purpose of wildlife-related recreation. Expenditures included both money spent by participants for themselves and the value of gifts they received.

Fishing—The sport of catching or attempting to catch fish with a hook and line, bow and arrow, or spear; it also includes catching or gathering shellfish (clams, crabs, etc.); and the noncommercial seining or netting of fish, unless the fish are for use as bait. For example, seining for smelt is fishing, but seining for bait minnows is not included as fishing.

Fishing equipment—Items owned primarily for fishing:

Rods, reels, poles, and rodmaking components

Lines and leaders

Artificial lures, flies, baits, and dressing for flies or lines

Hooks, sinkers, swivels, and other items attached to a line, except lures and baits

Tackle boxes

Creels, stringers, fish bags, landing nets, and gaff hooks

Minnow traps, seines, and bait containers

Depth finders, fish finders, and other electronic fishing devices

Ice fishing equipment

Other fishing equipment

Freshwater—Reservoirs, lakes, ponds, and the nontidal portions of rivers and streams.

Great Lakes fishing—Fishing in Lakes Superior, Michigan, Huron, St. Clair, Erie, and Ontario, their connecting waters such as the St. Mary's River system, Detroit River, St. Clair River, and the Niagara River, and the St. Lawrence River south of the bridge at Cornwall, New York. Great Lakes fishing includes fishing in tributaries of the Great Lakes for smelt, steelhead, and salmon.

Home—The starting point of a wildlife-related recreational trip. It may be a permanent residence or a temporary or seasonal residence such as a cabin.

Hunting—The sport of shooting or attempting to shoot wildlife with firearms or archery equipment.

Hunting equipment—Items owned primarily for hunting:

Rifles, shotguns, muzzleloaders, and handguns

Archery equipment

Telescopic sights

Decoys and game calls

Ammunition

Hand loading equipment

Hunting dogs and associated costs

Other hunting equipment

Land leasing and owning—Leasing or owning land either singly or in cooperation with others for the primary purpose of fishing, hunting, or wildlife watching on it.

Maintain natural areas—To set aside 1/4 acre or more of natural environment, such as wood lots or open fields, for the primary purpose of benefiting wildlife.

Maintain plantings—To introduce or encourage the growth of food and cover plants for the primary purpose of benefiting wildlife.

Metropolitan Statistical Area (MSA)—A Metropolitan Statistical Area is a grouping of one or more counties or equivalent entities that contain at least one urbanized area of 50,000 or more inhabitants. The "Outside MSA" classification include census-defined Micropolitan Statistical Areas (or Micro areas). A Micro area is defined as a grouping of one or more counties or equivalent entities that contain at least one urban cluster of at least 10,000 but less than 50,000 inhabitants. Refer to <www.census.gov/population/metro/about/>, for a more detailed definition of the Metropolitan Statistical Area.

Migratory birds—Birds that regularly migrate from one region or climate to another such as ducks, geese, and doves and other birds that may be hunted.

Multiple responses—The term used to reflect the fact that individuals or their characteristics fall into more than one reporting category. An example of a big game hunter who hunted for deer and elk demonstrates the effect of multiple responses. In this case, adding the number of deer hunters (one) and elk hunters (one) would overstate the number of big game hunters (one) because deer and elk hunters are not

mutually exclusive categories. In contrast, for example, total participants is the sum of male and female participants, because "male" and "female" are mutually exclusive categories.

Nonresidents—Individuals who do not live in the State being reported. For example, a person living in Texas who watches whales in California is a nonresidential wildlife-watcher in California.

Nonresponse—A term used to reflect the fact that some Survey respondents provide incomplete sets of information. For example, a Survey respondent may have been unable to identify the primary type of hunting for which a gun was bought. Total hunting expenditure estimates will include the gun purchase, but it will not appear as spending for big game or any other type of hunting. Nonresponses result in reported totals that are greater than the sum of their parts.

Observe—To take special interest in or try to identify birds, fish or other wildlife.

Other animals—Coyotes, crows, foxes, groundhogs, prairie dogs, raccoons, alligators, and similar animals that can be legally hunted and are not classified as big game, small game, or migratory birds. They may be classified as unprotected or predatory animals by the State in which they are hunted. Feral pigs are classified as "other animals" in all States except Hawaii, where they are considered big game.

Participants—Individuals who engage in fishing, hunting, or a wildlife-watching activity. Unless otherwise stated, a person has to have hunted, fished, or wildlife watched in 2011 to be considered a participant.

Plantings—See "Maintain plantings."

Primary purpose—The principal motivation for an activity, trip, or expenditure.

Private land—Land owned by a business, nongovernmental organization, private individual, or a group of individuals such as an association or club.

Public land—Land that is owned by local governments (such as county parks and municipal watersheds),

State governments (such as State parks and wildlife management areas), or the federal government (such as National Forests, Recreational Areas, and Wildlife Refuges).

Residents—Individuals who lived in the State being reported. For example, a person who lives in California and watches whales in California is a residential wildlife watcher in California.

Rural—All territory, population, and housing units located outside of urbanized areas and urban clusters, as determined by the U.S. Census Bureau.

Saltwater—Oceans, tidal bays and sounds, and the tidal portions of rivers and streams.

Screening interviews—The first Survey contact with a sample household. Screening interviews are conducted with a household representative to identify respondents who are eligible for in-depth interviews. Screening interviews gather data such as age and sex about individuals in the households. Further information on screening interviews is available on page vii in the "Survey Background and Method" section of this report.

Small game—Grouse, pheasants, quail, rabbits, squirrels, and similar small animals for which States have small game seasons and bag limits.

Special equipment—Big-ticket equipment items that are owned primarily for wildlife-related recreation:

Bass boats

Other types of motor boats

Canoes and other types of nonmotor boats

Boat motors, boat trailer/hitches, and other boat accessories

Pickups, campers, vans, travel or tent trailers, motor homes, house trailers, recreational vehicles (RVs)

Cabins

Off-the-road vehicles such as trail bikes, all terrain vehicles (ATVs), dune buggies, four-wheelers, 4x4 vehicles, and snowmobiles

Other special equipment

Spenders—Individuals who spent money on fishing, hunting, or wildlife-watching activities or equipment and also participated in those activities.

Sportspersons—Individuals who engaged in fishing, hunting, or both.

Trip—An outing involving fishing, hunting, or wildlife watching. A trip may begin from an individual's principal residence or from another place, such as a vacation home or the home of a relative. A trip may last an hour, a day, or many days.

Type of fishing—There are three types of fishing: (1) freshwater except Great Lakes, (2) Great Lakes, and (3) saltwater.

Type of hunting—There are four types of hunting: (1) big game, (2) small game, (3) migratory bird, and (4) other animal.

Unspecified expenditure—An item that was purchased for use in both fishing and hunting, rather than primarily one or the other. Auxiliary equipment, special equipment, magazines and books, and membership dues and contributions are the items for which a purchase could be categorized as "unspecified."

Urban—All territory, population, and housing units located within boundaries that encompass densely settled territory, consisting of core census block groups or blocks that have a population density of at least 1,000 people per square mile and surrounding census blocks that have an overall density of at least 500 people per square mile. Under certain conditions, less densely settled territory may be included, as determined by the Census Bureau.

Visit parks or natural areas—A visit to places accessible to the public and that are owned or leased by a governmental entity, nongovernmental organization, business, or a private individual or group such as an association or club.

Wildlife—Animals such as birds, fish, insects, mammals, amphibians, and reptiles that are living in natural or wild environments. Wildlife does not include animals living in aquariums, zoos, and other artificial surroundings or domestic animals such as farm animals or pets.

Wildlife observed, photographed, or fed—Examples of species that wildlife watchers observe, photograph, and/or feed are (1) *Wild birds*—songbirds such as cardinals, robins, warblers, jays, buntings, and sparrows; birds of prey such as hawks, owls, eagles, and falcons; waterfowl such as ducks, geese, and swans; other water birds such as shorebirds, herons, pelicans, and cranes; and other birds such as pheasants, turkeys, road runners, and woodpeckers; (2) *Land mammals*—large land mammals such as bears, bison, deer, moose, and elk; small land mammals such as squirrels, foxes, prairie dogs, and rabbits; (3) *Fish* such as salmon, sharks, and groupers; (4) *Marine mammals* such as whales, dolphins, and manatees; and (5) *Other wildlife* such as butterflies, turtles, spiders, and snakes.

Wildlife-related recreation—Recreational fishing, hunting, and wildlife watching.

Wildlife watching—There are six types of wildlife watching: (1) closely observing, (2) photographing, (3) feeding, (4) visiting parks or natural areas, (5) maintaining plantings, and (6) maintaining natural areas. These activities must be the primary purpose of the trip or the around-the-home undertaking.

Wildlife-watching equipment—Items owned primarily for observing, photographing, or feeding wildlife:

Binoculars and spotting scopes

Cameras, video cameras, special lenses, and other photographic equipment

Film and developing

Commercially prepared and packaged wild bird food

Other bulk food used to feed wild birds

Food for other wildlife

Nest boxes, bird houses, feeders, and baths

Day packs, carrying cases, and special clothing

Other items such as field guides and maps

Appendix B

Appendix B.
2010 Participation of 6- to 15-Year-Olds: Data From Screening Interviews

The 2011 National Survey of Fishing, Hunting, and Wildlife-Associated Recreation was carried out in two phases. The first (or screening) phase began in April 2011. The main purpose of this phase was to collect information about all persons 16 years old and older in order to develop a sample of potential sportspersons and wildlife watchers for the second (or detailed) phase. However, information was also collected on the number of persons 6 to 15 years old who participated in wildlife-related recreation activities in 2010.

It is important to emphasize that the information reported from the 2011 screen relates to activity only up to and including 2010. Also, these data are reported by one household respondent

speaking for all household members rather than the actual participants. In addition, these data are based on long-term recall (at least a 12-month recall), which has been found in Survey research (see *Investigation of Possible Recall/Reference Period Bias in National Surveys of Fishing, Hunting and Wildlife-Associated Recreation, December 1989, Westat, Inc.*) to add bias to the resulting estimates. In many cases, longer recall periods result in overestimating participation and expenditures for wildlife-related recreation.

Tables B-1 through B-4 report data on 6- to 15-year-old participants in 2010. Detailed expenditures and recreational activity data were not gathered for the 6- to 15-year-old participants.

Because of differences in methodologies of the screening and the detailed phases of the 2011 Survey, the estimates of the two phases are not comparable. Only participants 16 years old and older were eligible for the detailed phase. The screening phase covered activity for 2010 or earlier; the detailed phase has estimates for only 2011. The detailed phase was a series of interviews of the actual participants conducted at 4- and 8-month intervals. The screening phase was a single interview of one household respondent who reported household events with one year or more recall. The shorter recall period of the detailed phase enabled better data accuracy.

Table B-1. Texas Residents 6 to 15 Years Old Participating in Fishing and Hunting Both Inside and Outside Texas: 2010

(Population 6 to 15 years old. Numbers in thousands)

Sportspersons	Sportspersons 6 to 15 years old		
	Number	Percent of sportspersons	Percent of population
Total sportspersons..................	672	100	17
Total anglers	666	99	17
Fished only	504	75	13
Fished and hunted	*161	*24	*4
Total hunters	*167	*25	*4
Hunted only			
Hunted and fished	*161	*24	*4

* Estimate based on a sample size of 10–29   Sample size too small (less than 10) to report data reliably

Note: Detail does not add to total because of multiple responses Column showing percent of sportspersons is based on the "Total sportspersons" row Column showing percent of population is based on the state population 6 to 15 years old, including those who did not fish or hunt Data reported on this table are from screening interviews in which one adult household member responded for household members 6 to 15 years old The screening interview required the respondent to recall 12 months worth of activity Includes state residents who fished or hunted only in other countries

Table B-2. Selected Characteristics of Texas Resident Anglers and Hunters 6 to 15 Years Old: 2010

(Population 6 to 15 years old. Numbers in thousands)

Characteristic	Population		Sportspersons (fished or hunted)			Anglers			Hunters		
	Number	Percent	Number	Percent who par-ticipated	Percent	Number	Percent who par-ticipated	Percent	Number	Percent who par-ticipated	Percent
Total persons	**3,846**	**100**	**672**	**17**	**100**	**666**	**17**	**100**	***167**	***4**	***100**
Population Density of Residence											
Urban	2,849	74	*401	*14	*60	*401	*14	*60			
Rural	997	26	*271	*27	*40	*265	*27	*40	*135	*14	*81
Population Size of Residence											
Metropolitan Statistical Area (MSA)	3,806	99	646	17	96	646	17	97	*155	*4	*93
1,000,000 or more	2,748	71	*420	*15	*63	*420	*15	*63			
250,000 to 999,999	*417	*11									
50,000 to 249,999	642	17	*154	*24	*23	*154	*24	*23			
Outside MSA											
Age											
6 to 8 years	1,125	29	*170	*15	*25	*170	*15	*26			
9 to 11 years	1,696	44	*309	*18	*46	*309	*18	*46			
12 to 15 years	1,025	27	*193	*19	*29	*187	*18	*28			
Sex											
Male	1,978	51	*385	*19	*57	*379	*19	*57	*147	*7	*88
Female	1,867	49	*286	*15	*43	*286	*15	*43			
Ethnicity											
Hispanic	1,274	33	*244	*19	*36	*244	*19	*37			
Non-Hispanic	2,572	67	428	17	64	422	16	63	*158	*6	*94
Race											
White	2,826	73	529	19	79	523	19	79	*132	*5	*79
African American	*311	*8									
All others	*709	*18									
Annual Household Income											
Less than $20,000	*773	*20									
$20,000 to $29,999	*564	*15									
$30,000 to $39,999	*386	*10									
$40,000 to $49,999											
$50,000 to $74,999	*802	*21									
$75,000 to $99,999	*440	*11									
$100,000 or more	*473	*12	*209	*44	*31	*209	*44	*31			
Not reported	*242	*6									

* Estimate based on a sample size of 10–29   Sample size too small (less than 10) to report data reliably

Note: Percent who participated columns show the percent of each row's population who participated in the activity named by the column (the percent of those living in urban areas who wildlife watched, etc) Remaining percent columns show the percent of each column's participants who are described by the row heading (the percent of wildlife watchers who lived in urban areas, etc) Data reported on this table are from screening interviews in which one adult household member responded for household members 6 to 15 years old The screening interview required the respondent to recall 12 months worth of activity Includes state residents who wildlife watched only in other countries

Table B-3. Texas Residents 6 to 15 Years Old Participating in Wildlife Watching Both Inside and Outside Texas: 2010

(Population 6 to 15 years old. Numbers in thousands)

Participants	Number	Percent of participants	Percent of population
Total participants	1,112	100	29
Away from home	*318	*29	*8
Around the home	989	89	26
Observe wildlife	941	85	24
Photograph wildlife			
Feed wild birds or other wildlife	*406	*36	*11
Maintain plantings or natural areas			

* Estimate based on a sample size of 10–29   ... Sample size too small (less than 10) to report data reliably

Note: Detail does not add to total because of multiple responses The column showing percent of participation is based on total participants The column showing percent of population is based on the state population 6 to 15 years old, including those who did not participate in wildlife watching Data reported on this table are from screening interviews in which one adult household member responded for all household members 6 to 15 years old The screening interview required the respondent to recall 12 months worth of activity Includes persons who wildlife watched only in other countries

Table B-4. Selected Characteristics of Texas Resident Wildlife Watchers 6 to 15 Years Old: 2010

(Population 6 to 15 years old. Numbers in thousands)

Characteristic	Population		Total wildlife watchers			Away from Home			Around the home		
	Number	Percent	Number	Percent who participated	Percent	Number	Percent who participated	Percent	Number	Percent who participated	Percent
Total persons	3,846	100	1,112	29	100	*318	*8	*100	989	26	100
Population Density of Residence											
Urban	2,849	74	674	24	61	*200	*7	*63	*557	*20	*56
Rural	997	26	*437	*44	*39				*431	*43	*44
Population Size of Residence											
Metropolitan Statistical Area (MSA)	3,806	99	1,100	29	99	*312	*8	*98	983	26	99
1,000,000 or more	2,748	71	872	32	78	*209	*8	*66	*786	*29	*80
250,000 to 999,999	*417	*11									
50,000 to 249,999	642	17	*141	*22	*13						
Outside MSA											
Age											
6 to 8 years	1,125	29									
9 to 11 years	1,696	44	*757	*45	*68				*705	*42	*71
12 to 15 years	1,025	27	*242	*24	*22				*210	*21	*21
Sex											
Male	1,978	51	*648	*33	*58	*237	*12	*75	*551	*28	*56
Female	1,867	49	*464	*25	*42				*438	*23	*44
Ethnicity											
Hispanic	1,274	33	*193	*15	*17				*164	*13	*17
Non-Hispanic	2,572	67	918	36	83	*260	*10	*82	*825	*32	*83
Race											
White	2,826	73	1,021	36	92	*290	*10	*91	898	32	91
African American	*311	*8									
All others	*709	*18									
Annual Household Income											
Less than $20,000	*773	*20									
$20,000 to $29,999	*564	*15									
$30,000 to $39,999	*386	*10									
$40,000 to $49,999											
$50,000 to $74,999	*802	*21									
$75,000 to $99,999	*440	*11									
$100,000 or more	*473	*12									
Not reported	*242	*6									

* Estimate based on a sample size of 10–29   Sample size too small (less than 10) to report data reliably

Note: Percent who participated columns show the percent of each row's population who participated in the activity named by the column (the percent of those living in urban areas who fished, etc) Remaining percent columns show the percent of each column's participants who are described by the row heading (the percent of anglers who lived in urban areas, etc) Data reported on this table are from screening interviews in which one adult household member responded for household members 6 to 15 years old The screening interview required the respondent to recall 12 months worth of activity Includes state residents who fished or hunted only in other countries

Appendix C

Appendix C.
Significant Methodological Changes From Previous Surveys and Regional Trends

This appendix provides a description of data collection changes and national and regional trend information based on the 1991, 1996, 2001, 2006, and 2011 Surveys. Since these five surveys used similar methodologies, their published information is directly comparable.

Significant Methodological Differences

The most significant design differences in the five Surveys are as follows:

1. The 1991 Survey data was collected by interviewers filling out paper questionnaires. The data entries were keyed in a separate operation after the interview. The 1996, 2001, 2006, and 2011 Survey data were collected by the use of computer-assisted interviews. The questionnaires were programmed into computers, and the interviewer keyed in the responses at the time of the interview.

2. The 1991 Survey screening phase was conducted in January and February of 1991, when a household member of the sample households was interviewed on behalf of the entire household. The screening interviews for the 1996, 2001, and 2006 Surveys were conducted April through June of their survey years in conjunction with the first wave of the detailed interviews. The 2011 Survey also conducted screening interviews and the first detailed interviews April through June of 2011, but furthermore had an additional screening and detailed effort from February 2012 to the end of May 2012. The April–June 2011 screening effort had a high noncontact rate because of poor results using sample telephone numbers obtained from a private firm. Census went back to

the noncontacted component of the original sample in February-May 2012 and interviewed a subsample, requiring annual recall for those respondents. The Wave 3 screen sample was 12,484 of the total 48,600 household screen sample. A modification of the 2011 sampling scheme was to oversample counties that had relatively high proportions of hunting license purchases.

The screening interviews for all five Surveys consisted primarily of demographic questions and wildlife-related recreation questions concerning activity in the previous year (1990, 1995, etc.) and intentions for recreating in the survey year.

In the 1991 Survey, an attempt was made to contact every sample person in all three detailed interview waves. In 1996, 2001, 2006, and 2011 respondents who were interviewed in the first detailed interview wave were not contacted again until the third wave (unless they were part of the other subsample, i.e., a respondent in both the sportsperson and wildlife watching subsamples could be in the first and third wave of sportsperson interviewing and the second and third wave of wildlife watching interviewing). Also, all interviews in the second wave were conducted only by telephone. In-person interviews were only conducted in the first and third waves. The 2011 wave 3 screen phase was composed of both telephone and in-person interviews.

Section I. Important Instrument Changes in the 1996 Survey

1. The 1991 Survey collected information on all wildlife-related recreation purchases made by participants without reference to where the purchase was made. The

1996 Survey asked in which state the purchase was made.

2. In 1991, respondents were asked what kind of fishing they did, i.e., Great Lakes, other freshwater, or saltwater, and then were asked in what states they fished. In 1996, respondents were asked in which states they fished and then were asked what kind of fishing they did. This method had the advantage of not asking about, for example, saltwater fishing when they only fished in a noncoastal state.

3. In 1991, respondents were asked how many days they "actually" hunted or fished for a particular type of game or fish and then how many days they "chiefly" hunted or fished for the same type of game or fish rather than another type of game or fish. To get total days of hunting or fishing for a particular type of game or fish, the "actually" day response was used, while to get the sum of all days of hunting or fishing, the "chiefly" days were summed. In 1996, respondents were asked their total days of hunting or fishing in the country and each state, then how many days they hunted or fished for a particular type of game or fish.

4. Trip-related and equipment expenditure categories were not the same for all Surveys. "Guide fee" and "Pack trip or package fee" were two separate trip-related expenditure items in 1991, while they were combined into one category in the 1996 Survey. "Boating costs" was added to the 1996 hunting and wildlife-watching trip-related expenditure sections. "Heating and cooking fuel" was added to all of the trip-related expenditure sections. "Spearfishing equipment"

was moved from a separate category to the "other" list. "Rods" and "Reels" were two separate categories in 1991 but were combined in 1996. "Lines, hooks, sinkers, etc." was one category in 1991 but split into "Lines" and "Hooks, sinkers, etc." in 1996. "Food used to feed other wildlife" was added to the wildlife-watching equipment section, "Boats" and "Cabins" were added to the wildlife-watching special equipment section, and "Land leasing and ownership" was added to the wildlife-watching expenditures section.

5. Questions asking sportspersons if they participated as much as they wanted were added in 1996. If the sportspersons said no, they were asked why not.

6. The 1991 Survey included questions about participation in organized fishing competitions; anglers using bows and arrows, nets or seines, or spearfishing; hunters using pistols or handguns and target shooting in preparation for hunting. These questions were not asked in 1996.

7. The 1996 Survey included questions about catch and release fishing and persons with disabilities participating in wildlife-related recreation. These questions were not part of the 1991 Survey.

8. The 1991 Survey included questions about average distance traveled to recreation sites. These questions were not included in the 1996 Survey.

9. The 1996 Survey included questions about the last trip the respondent took. Included were questions about the type of trip, where the activity took place, and the distance and direction to the site visited. These questions were not asked in 1991.

10. The 1991 Survey collected data on hunting, fishing, and wildlife watching by U.S. residents in Canada. The 1996 Survey collected data on fishing and wildlife-watching by U.S. residents in Canada.

Section II. Important Instrument Changes in the 2001 Survey

1. The 1991 and 1996 single race category "Asian or Pacific Islander" was changed to two categories "Asian" and "Native Hawaiian or Other Pacific Islander." In 1991 and 1996, the respondent was required to pick only one category, while in 2001 the respondent could pick any combination of categories. The next question stipulated that the respondent could only be identified with one category and then asked what that category was.

2. The 1991 and 1996 land leasing and ownership sections asked the respondent to combine the two types of land use into one and give total acreage and expenditures. In 2001, the two types of land use were explored separately.

3. The 1991 and 1996 wildlife-watching sections included questions on birdwatching for around-the-home participants only. The 2001 Survey added a question on birdwatching for away-from-home participants. Also, questions on the use of birding life lists and how many species the respondent can identify were added.

4. "Recreational vehicles" was added to the sportspersons and wildlife-watchers special equipment section. "House trailer" was added to the sportspersons special equipment section.

5. Total personal income was asked in the detailed phase of the 1996 Survey. This was changed to total household income in the 2001 Survey.

6. A question was added to the trip-related expenditures section to ascertain how much of the total was spent in the respondent's state of residence when the respondent participated in hunting, fishing, or wildlife watching out-of-state.

7. Boating questions were added to the fishing section. The respondent was asked about the extent of boat usage for the three types of fishing.

8. The 1996 Survey included questions about the months around-the-home wildlife watchers fed birds. These questions were not repeated in the 2001 Survey.

9. The contingent valuation sections of the three types of wildlife-related recreation were altered, using an open-ended question format instead of 1996's dichotomous choice format.

Section III. Important Instrument Changes in the 2006 Survey

1. A series of boating questions was added. The new questions dealt with anglers using motorboats and/or nonmotorboats, length of boat used most often, distance to boat launch used most often, needed improvements to facilities at the launch, whether or not the respondent completed a boating safety course, who the boater fished with most often, and the source and type of information the boater used for his or her fishing.

2. Questions regarding catch and release fishing were added. They were whether or not the respondent caught and released fish and, if so, the percent of fish released.

3. The proportion of hunting done with a rifle or shotgun, as contrasted with muzzleloader or archery equipment, was asked.

4. In the contingent valuation section, where the value of wildlife-related recreation was determined, two quality-variable questions were added: the average length of certain fish caught and whether a deer, elk, or moose was killed. Plus the economic evaluation bid questions were rephrased, from "What is the most your [species] hunting in [State name] could have cost you per trip last year before you would NOT have gone [species] hunting at all in 2001, not even one trip, because it would have been too expensive?", for the hunters, for example, to "What is the cost that would have prevented you from taking even one such trip in 2006? In other words, if the trip cost was below this amount, you would have gone [species] hunting in [State name], but if the trip cost was above this amount, you would not have gone."

5. Questions concerning hunting, fishing, or wildlife watching in other countries were taken out of the Survey.

6. Questions about the reasons for not going hunting or fishing, or not going as much as expected, were deleted.

7. Disability of participants questions were taken out.

8. Determination of the types of sites for wildlife watching was discontinued.

9. The birding questions regarding the use of birding life lists and the ability to identify birds based on their sight or sounds were deleted.

10. Public transportation costs were divided into two sections, "public transportation by airplane" and "other public transportation, including trains, buses, and car rentals, etc.".

Section IV. Important Instrument Changes in the 2011 Survey

1. The series of boating questions added in 2006 was deleted.

2. Questions about target shooting and the usage of a shooting range in preparation for hunting were added. The types of weapon used at the shooting range were quantified.

3. Questions about plantings expenditures for the purpose of hunting were added.

4. "Feral pig" was recategorized from big game to other animals for all states except Hawaii.

5. "Ptarmigan" was included as its own small game category, instead of lumped in "other."

6. In previous Surveys, "Moose" was included as its own category only for Alaska. For 2011, "Moose" was included as its own big game category, instead of lumped in "other," for all fifty states.

7. In previous Surveys, "Wolf" was included as its own category only for Alaska. For 2011, "Wolf" was included as its own other animal category, instead of lumped in "other," for all fifty states.

8. The household income categories were modified. The top categories were changed from "$100,000 or more" to "$100,000 to $149,999" and "$150,000 or more."

9. The "Steelhead" category was deleted from the saltwater fish species section, with the idea that it would be included in "other."

10. The 2006 around-the-home wildlife-watching category that quantified visitors of "public parks or areas" was rewritten to wildlife watching at "parks or natural areas." This change was to make clear that respondents should include recreating at quasi-governmental and private areas.

11. The 2006 wildlife watching equipment category "Film and developing" was rewritten to "Film and photo processing."

Regional Trends

This trends section covers the period from 1991 to 2011. The 1991, 1996, 2001, 2006, and 2011 Surveys used similar methodologies, making all published information for the five Surveys directly comparable.

Table C-1a. Comparison of Wildlife-Related Recreation in the United States: 1991–1996

(U.S. population 16 years old and older. Numbers in thousands. All expenditures in 2011 dollars. 1996 expenditures categories made comparable to 1991)

Participants, days, and expenditures	1991 (number)	1996 (number)	1991–1996 percent change
Hunting			
Hunters, total	14,063	13,975	NS_1
Hunting days, total	235,806	256,676	NS0
Hunting expenditures, total	$20,399,152	$29,259,999	43
Fishing			
Anglers, total	35,578	35,246	NS_1
Fishing days, total	511,329	625,893	22
Fishing expenditures, total	$39,669,337	$54,224,581	37
Wildlife Watching			
Wildlife watchers, total	76,111	62,868	−17
Around the home	73,904	60,751	−18
Away from home	29,999	23,652	−21
Wildlife-watching days, away from home	342,406	313,790	NS_8
Wildlife-watching expenditures, total	$30,574,499	$36,924,875	21

NS Not different from zero at the 5 percent level of significance

Table C-1b. Comparison of Wildlife-Related Recreation in the United States: 1996–2001

(U.S. population 16 years old and older. Numbers in thousands. All expenditures in 2011 dollars. 1996 and 2001 expenditures categories made comparable to 1991)

Participants, days, and expenditures	1996 (number)	2001 (number)	1996–2001 percent change
Hunting			
Hunters, total	13,975	13,034	−7
Hunting days, total	256,676	228,368	−11
Hunting expenditures, total	$29,259,999	$25,993,960	NS_11
Fishing			
Anglers, total	35,246	34,071	−3
Fishing days, total	625,893	557,394	−11
Fishing expenditures, total	$54,224,581	$45,076,739	−17
Wildlife Watching			
Wildlife watchers, total	62,868	66,105	5
Around the home	60,751	62,928	4
Away from home	23,652	21,823	−8
Wildlife-watching days, away from home	313,790	372,006	19
Wildlife-watching expenditures, total	$36,924,875	$42,904,872	16

NS Not different from zero at the 5 percent level of significance

Table C-1c. Comparison of Wildlife-Related Recreation in the United States: 2001–2006

(U.S. population 16 years old and older. Numbers in thousands. All expenditures in 2011 dollars. 2001 and 2006 expenditures categories made comparable to 1991)

Participants, days, and expenditures	2001 (number)	2006 (number)	2001–2006 percent change
Hunting			
Hunters, total	13,034	12,510	NS_4
Hunting days, total	228,368	219,925	NS_4
Hunting expenditures, total	$25,993,960	$25,265,523	NS_3
Fishing			
Anglers, total	34,071	29,952	−12
Fishing days, total	557,394	516,781	−7
Fishing expenditures, total	$45,076,739	$46,909,364	NS4
Wildlife Watching			
Wildlife watchers, total	66,105	71,132	8
Around the home	62,928	67,756	8
Away from home	21,823	22,977	NS5
Wildlife-watching days, away from home	372,006	352,070	NS_5
Wildlife-watching expenditures, total	$42,904,872	$40,023,078	NS_7

NS Not different from zero at the 5 percent level of significance

Table C-1d. Comparison of Wildlife-Related Recreation in the United States: 2006–2011

(U.S. population 16 years old and older. Numbers in thousands. All expenditures in 2011 dollars. 2006 and 2011 expenditures categories made comparable to 1991)

Participants, days, and expenditures	2006 (number)	2011 (number)	2006–2011 percent change
Hunting			
Hunters, total	12,510	13,674	9
Hunting days, total	219,925	281,884	28
Hunting expenditures, total	$25,265,523	$32,579,640	29
Fishing			
Anglers, total	29,952	33,112	11
Fishing days, total	516,781	553,841	NS7
Fishing expenditures, total	$46,909,364	$41,624,599	NS_11
Wildlife Watching			
Wildlife watchers, total	71,132	71,776	NS1
Around the home	67,756	68,598	NS1
Away from home	22,977	22,496	NS_2
Wildlife-watching days, away from home	352,070	335,625	NS_5
Wildlife-watching expenditures, total	$40,023,078	$43,636,608	NS9

NS Not different from zero at the 5 percent level of significance

Table C-1e. Comparison of Wildlife-Related Recreation in the United States: 1991–2011

(U.S. population 16 years old and older. Numbers in thousands. All expenditures in 2011 dollars. 2011 expenditures categories made comparable to 1991)

Participants, days, and expenditures	1991 (number)	2011 (number)	1991–2011 percent change
Hunting			
Hunters, total	14,063	13,674	[NS]-3
Hunting days, total	235,806	281,884	20
Hunting expenditures, total	$20,399,152	$32,579,640	60
Fishing			
Anglers, total	35,578	33,112	-7
Fishing days, total	511,329	553,841	8
Fishing expenditures, total	$39,669,337	$41,624,599	[NS]5
Wildlife Watching			
Wildlife watchers, total	76,111	71,776	-6
Around the home	73,904	68,598	-7
Away from home	29,999	22,496	-25
Wildlife-watching days, away from home	342,406	335,625	[NS]-2
Wildlife-watching expenditures, total	$30,574,499	$43,636,608	43

[NS] Not different from zero at the 5 percent level of significance

Table C-2. Anglers and Hunters by Census Division: 1991, 1996, 2001, 2006, and 2011

(U.S. population 16 years old and older. Numbers in thousands)

Area and sportsperson	1991 Number	1991 Percent	1996 Number	1996 Percent	2001 Number	2001 Percent	2006 Number	2006 Percent	2011 Number	2011 Percent
UNITED STATES										
Total population	189,964	100	201,472	100	212,298	100	229,245	100	239,313	100
Sportspersons	39,979	21	39,694	20	37,805	18	33,916	15	37,397	16
Anglers	35,578	19	35,246	17	34,067	16	29,952	13	33,112	14
Hunters	14,063	7	13,975	7	13,034	6	12,510	5	13,674	6
New England										
Total population	10,180	100	10,306	100	10,575	100	11,233	100	11,593	100
Sportspersons	1,658	16	1,673	16	1,504	14	1,353	12	1,441	12
Anglers	1,545	15	1,520	15	1,402	13	1,246	11	1,355	12
Hunters	444	4	465	5	386	4	374	3	420	4
Middle Atlantic										
Total population	29,216	100	29,371	100	29,806	100	31,518	100	32,392	100
Sportspersons	4,508	15	4,192	14	3,810	13	3,214	10	3,966	12
Anglers	3,871	13	3,627	12	3,250	11	2,550	8	3,496	11
Hunters	1,746	6	1,453	5	1,633	5	1,520	5	1,558	5
East North Central										
Total population	32,188	100	33,121	100	34,082	100	35,609	100	36,199	100
Sportspersons	7,202	22	6,912	21	6,400	19	5,975	17	6,766	19
Anglers	6,264	19	6,006	18	5,655	17	5,190	15	5,861	16
Hunters	2,789	9	2,712	8	2,421	7	2,376	7	2,688	7
West North Central										
Total population	13,504	100	13,875	100	14,430	100	15,458	100	15,860	100
Sportspersons	4,143	31	3,977	29	4,239	29	3,836	25	3,980	25
Anglers	3,647	27	3,416	25	3,836	27	3,284	21	3,591	23
Hunters	1,709	13	1,917	14	1,710	12	1,779	12	1,661	10
South Atlantic										
Total population	33,682	100	36,776	100	39,286	100	43,965	100	46,417	100
Sportspersons	6,996	21	7,282	20	6,957	18	6,633	15	6,749	15
Anglers	6,441	19	6,636	18	6,451	16	6,116	14	6,163	13
Hunters	2,083	6	2,050	6	1,875	5	1,884	4	1,870	4
East South Central										
Total population	11,667	100	12,459	100	12,976	100	13,722	100	14,206	100
Sportspersons	2,984	26	2,907	23	2,865	22	2,689	20	3,010	21
Anglers	2,635	23	2,514	20	2,543	20	2,436	18	2,444	17
Hunters	1,279	11	1,301	10	1,164	9	1,101	8	1,531	11
West South Central										
Total population	19,926	100	21,811	100	23,337	100	25,407	100	27,195	100
Sportspersons	5,125	26	5,093	23	4,924	21	4,499	18	4,855	18
Anglers	4,592	23	4,616	21	4,375	19	3,952	16	4,298	16
Hunters	1,843	9	1,812	8	1,988	9	1,810	7	1,909	7
Mountain										
Total population	10,092	100	11,966	100	13,308	100	15,651	100	17,013	100
Sportspersons	2,488	25	2,761	23	2,757	21	2,372	15	2,976	17
Anglers	2,079	21	2,411	20	2,443	18	2,084	13	2,586	15
Hunters	1,069	11	1,061	9	1,020	8	868	6	1,043	6
Pacific										
Total population	29,508	100	31,787	100	34,498	100	36,681	100	38,438	100
Sportspersons	4,875	17	4,897	15	4,349	13	3,345	9	3,654	10
Anglers	4,505	15	4,501	14	4,111	12	3,094	8	3,319	9
Hunters	1,101	4	1,203	4	837	2	798	2	996	3

Table C-3.   Wildlife-Watching Participants by Census Division: 1991, 1996, 2001, 2006, and 2011

(U.S. population 16 years old and older. Numbers in thousands)

Area and wildlife watcher	1991 Number	1991 Percent	1996 Number	1996 Percent	2001 Number	2001 Percent	2006 Number	2006 Percent	2011 Number	2011 Percent
UNITED STATES										
Total population	189,964	100	201,472	100	212,298	100	229,245	100	239,313	100
Total wildlife watchers	76,111	40	62,868	31	66,105	31	71,132	31	71,776	30
Away from home	29,999	16	23,652	12	21,823	10	22,977	10	22,496	9
Around the home	73,904	39	60,751	30	62,928	30	67,756	30	68,598	29
New England										
Total population	10,180	100	10,306	100	10,575	100	11,233	100	11,593	100
Total wildlife watchers	4,598	45	3,710	36	3,875	37	4,489	40	3,954	34
Away from home	1,856	18	1,443	14	1,155	11	1,340	12	1,187	10
Around the home	4,544	45	3,586	35	3,765	36	4,310	38	3,858	33
Middle Atlantic										
Total population	29,216	100	29,371	100	29,806	100	31,518	100	32,392	100
Total wildlife watchers	10,556	36	8,185	28	8,740	29	8,723	28	9,118	28
Away from home	4,166	14	2,960	10	2,849	10	2,729	9	2,561	8
Around the home	10,282	35	8,023	27	8,452	28	8,451	27	8,744	27
East North Central										
Total population	32,188	100	33,121	100	34,082	100	35,609	100	36,199	100
Total wildlife watchers	14,511	45	11,731	35	11,631	34	12,215	34	12,840	35
Away from home	5,572	17	4,501	14	3,571	10	3,792	11	3,168	9
Around the home	14,175	44	11,297	34	11,196	33	11,845	33	12,492	35
West North Central										
Total population	13,504	100	13,875	100	14,430	100	15,458	100	15,860	100
Total wildlife watchers	6,924	51	5,089	37	6,206	43	6,741	44	5,479	35
Away from home	2,654	20	1,927	14	2,059	14	2,163	14	1,783	11
Around the home	6,722	50	4,900	35	5,938	41	6,447	42	5,201	33
South Atlantic										
Total population	33,682	100	36,776	100	39,286	100	43,965	100	46,417	100
Total wildlife watchers	13,047	39	11,252	31	11,395	29	12,862	29	13,315	29
Away from home	4,450	13	3,992	11	3,469	9	3,208	7	4,393	9
Around the home	12,813	38	10,964	30	10,911	28	12,432	28	12,767	28
East South Central										
Total population	11,667	100	12,459	100	12,976	100	13,722	100	14,206	100
Total wildlife watchers	4,864	42	3,904	31	4,514	35	4,931	36	4,663	33
Away from home	1,592	14	1,118	9	1,086	8	1,758	13	1,456	10
Around the home	4,765	41	3,795	30	4,390	34	4,683	34	4,394	31
West South Central										
Total population	19,926	100	21,811	100	23,337	100	25,407	100	27,195	100
Total wildlife watchers	7,035	35	5,933	27	5,747	25	6,764	27	7,164	26
Away from home	2,459	12	2,096	10	1,822	8	2,127	8	1,728	6
Around the home	6,817	34	5,773	26	5,490	24	6,319	25	7,087	26
Mountain										
Total population	10,092	100	11,966	100	13,308	100	15,651	100	17,013	100
Total wildlife watchers	4,437	44	4,099	34	4,619	35	4,968	32	5,189	30
Away from home	2,215	22	1,967	16	2,019	15	2,004	13	2,230	13
Around the home	4,145	41	3,855	32	4,282	32	4,605	29	4,716	28
Pacific										
Total population	29,508	100	31,787	100	34,498	100	36,681	100	38,438	100
Total wildlife watchers	10,139	34	8,966	28	9,377	27	9,439	26	10,054	26
Away from home	5,035	17	3,648	11	3,793	11	3,856	11	3,990	10
Around the home	9,641	33	8,558	27	8,504	25	8,664	24	9,337	24

Appendix D

Appendix D.
Sample Design and Statistical Accuracy

This appendix is presented in two parts. The first part is the U.S. Census Bureau Source and Accuracy Statement. This statement describes the sampling design for the 2011 Survey and highlights the steps taken to produce estimates from the completed questionnaires. The statement explains the use of standard errors and confidence intervals. It also provides comprehensive information about errors characteristic of surveys and formulas and parameters to calculate an approximate standard error or confidence interval for each number published in this report. The second part, Tables D-1 and D-2, reports estimates and approximate standard errors for selected measures of participation and expenditures for wildlife-related recreation.

Source and Accuracy Statement for the Texas State Report of the *2011 National Survey of Fishing, Hunting, and Wildlife-Associated Recreation*

SOURCE OF DATA

The estimates in this report are based on data collected in the *2011 National Survey of Fishing, Hunting, and Wildlife-Associated Recreation* (FHWAR) conducted by the Census Bureau and sponsored by the U.S. Fish and Wildlife Service.

The eligible universe for the FHWAR is the civilian noninstitutionalized and nonbarrack military population living in the United States. The institutionalized population, which is excluded from the population universe, is composed primarily of the population in correctional institutions and nursing homes (98 percent of the 4 million institutionalized people in Census 2010).

The 2011 FHWAR was designed to provide state-level estimates of the number of participants in recreational

hunting and fishing and in wildlife watching activities (e.g., wildlife observation). Information was collected on the number of participants, where and how often they participated, the type of wildlife encountered, and the amounts of money spent on wildlife-related recreation.

The survey was conducted in two stages: an initial screening of households to identify likely sportspersons and wildlife-watching participants and a series of follow-up interviews of selected persons to collect detailed data about their wildlife-related recreation during 2011.

SAMPLE DESIGN

The 2011 FHWAR sample was selected from the Census Bureau's master address file (MAF).

The FHWAR is a multistage probability sample, with coverage in all 50 states and the District of Columbia.[1] In the first stage of the sampling process, primary sampling units (PSUs) are selected for sample. The PSUs are defined to correspond to the Office of Management and Budget definitions of Core Based Statistical Area definitions and to improve efficiency in field operations. The United States is divided into 2,025 PSUs. These PSUs are grouped into 824 strata. Within each stratum, a single PSU is chosen for the sample, with its probability of selection proportional to its population as of the 2000 decennial census. This PSU represents the entire stratum from which it was selected. In the case of strata consisting of only one PSU, the PSU is chosen with certainty.

---

[1] The sample size in the District of Columbia (D C) is not of sufficient size to produce reliable estimates for only D C The sample responses from D C are included in the U S totals for complete coverage of the U S (excluding Puerto Rico and the U S Virgin Islands)

Within the selected PSUs, the FHWAR sample was selected from the MAF.

FHWAR Screening Sample

The total screening sample in Texas consisted of **721** households. Interviewing for the screen was conducted during April, May, and June 2011. Due to a high noncontact rate, an additional personal visit screening interview, for a subsample of noncontact cases, occurred again in February, March, April, or May 2012. Of all housing units in sample, about **612** were determined to be eligible for interview. Interviewers obtained interviews at **439** of these units for a Texas response rate of **72** percent.[2] Texas's weighted response rate was **77** percent. The interviewers asked screening questions for all household members 6 years old and older. Noninterviews occur when the occupants are not found at home after repeated calls or are unavailable for some other reason.

Data for the FHWAR sportspersons sample and wildlife-watchers sample were collected in three waves.[3] The first wave started in April 2011, the second in September 2011, and the third in January 2012. In the sportspersons sample, all persons who hunted or fished in 2011 by the time of the screening interview were interviewed in the first wave. The remaining sportspersons in sample were interviewed in the second wave. The reference period was the preceding 4 months for waves 1 and 2. In wave 3, the reference period was either 4, 8, or 12 months depending on when the sample person was first interviewed.

---

[2] Response rates are calculated by using APPOR's RR2 formula

[3] The sample cases selected due to high noncontact rates were only interviewed once They received a screener and if they had some form of participation a detailed questionnaire These participants did not get three waves of interviewing The reference period for these sampled cases was between 13 and 16 months

Detailed Samples

Two independent detailed samples were chosen from the FHWAR screening sample. One consisted of sportspersons (people who hunt or fish) and the other of wildlife watchers (people who observe, photograph, or feed wildlife).

A. Sportspersons

The Census Bureau selected the detailed samples based on information reported during the screening phase. Based on information collected from the household respondent, every person 16 years old and older in the FHWAR screening sample was assigned to a sportspersons stratum. The criteria for the strata included time devoted to hunting or fishing in previous years, participation in hunting or fishing in 2011 by the time of the screening interview, and intentions to participate in hunting and fishing activities during the remainder of 2011.[4] The four sportspersons categories were:

1. *Active*—a person who had already participated in hunting or fishing in 2011 at the time of the screener interview.

2. *Likely*—a person who had not participated in 2011 at the time of the screener, but had participated in 2010 OR was likely to participate in 2011.

3. *Inactive*—a person who had not participated in 2010 or 2011 AND was somewhat unlikely to participate in 2011.

4. *Nonparticipant*—a person who had not participated in 2010 or 2011 AND was very unlikely to participate in 2011.

Due to the high noncontact rates in wave 1, all persons in the active, likely, and inactive groups were selected with certainty.

Active sportspersons were given the detailed interview twice—at the time of the screening interview (in April, May, or June 2011) and again in January or February 2012.[5] Likely sportspersons and inactive sportspersons were also interviewed

twice—first in September or October 2011, then in January or February 2012. Persons in the nonparticipant group were not eligible for a detailed interview. About **205** persons were designated for interviews in Texas. The detailed sportspersons sample sizes varied by state to get reliable state-level estimates. During each interview period, about **20** percent of the designated persons were not found at home or were unavailable for some other reason. Overall, about **164** detailed sportspersons interviews were completed at a response rate of **80** percent.

B. Wildlife Watchers

The wildlife-watching detailed sample was also selected based on information reported during the screening phase. Based on information collected from the household respondent, every person 16 years old and older was assigned to a stratum. The criteria for the strata included time devoted to wildlife watching activities in previous years, participation in wildlife watching activities in 2011 by the time of the screening interview, and intentions to participate in wildlife watching activities during the remainder of 2011.[6] The five wildlife-watching categories were:

1. *Active*—a person who had already participated in 2011 at the time of the screening interview.

2. *Avid*—a person who had not yet participated in 2011, but in 2010 had taken trips to participate in wildlife-watching activities for 21 or more days or had spent $300 or more.

3. *Average*—a person who had not yet participated in 2011, but in 2010 had taken trips to wildlife watch for less than 21 days and had spent less than $300 OR had not participated in wildlife-watching activities but was very likely to in the remainder of 2011.

4. *Infrequent*—a person who had not participated in 2010 or 2011, but was somewhat

likely or somewhat unlikely to participate in the remainder of 2011.

5. *Nonparticipant*—a person who had not participated in 2010 or 2011 AND was very unlikely to participate during the remainder of 2011.

Persons were selected for the detailed sample based on these groupings, but persons in the nonparticipant group were not eligible for a detailed interview.

A subsample of each of the other groups was selected to receive a detailed interview with the chance of selection diminishing as the likelihood of participation diminished. Wildlife-watching participants were given the detailed interview twice.[7] Some received their first detailed interview at the same time as the screening interview (in April, May, or June 2011). The rest received their first detailed interview in September or October 2011. All wildlife-watching participants received their second interview in January or February 2012. Some respondents were given the screener and detailed interview in February, March, April, or May 2012. About **164** persons were designated for interviews in Texas. The detailed wildlife-watching sample sizes varied by state to get reliable state-level estimates. During each interview period, about **26** percent of the designated persons were not found at home or were unavailable for some other reason. Overall, about **122** detailed wildlife watcher interviews were completed at a response rate of **74** percent.

ESTIMATION PROCEDURE

Several stages of adjustments were used to derive the final 2011 FHWAR person weights. A brief description of the major components of the weights is given below. All statistics for the population 6 to 15 years of age were derived from the screening interview. Statistics for the population 16 years old and older come from both the screening and detailed interviews. Estimates that come from the screening sample are presented in Appendix B.

---

[4] The sample cases selected due to high noncontact rates were not assigned a sportsperson stratum

[5] The sample cases selected due to high noncontact rates were given the detailed sportsperson interview once

[6] The sample cases selected due to high noncontact rates were not assigned a wildlife watcher stratum Wildlife-watching participants in these cases were then subsampled into the detailed questionnaire

[7] The sample cases selected due to high noncontact rates were given the detailed wildlife-watching interview once

A. Screening Sample

Every interviewed person in the screening sample received a screening weight that was the product of the following factors:

1. *Base Weight.* The base weight is the inverse of the household's probability of selection.

2. *Household Noninterview Adjustment.* The noninterview adjustment inflates the weight assigned to interviewed households to account for households eligible for interview but for which no interview was obtained.

3. *First-Stage Adjustment.* The 824 areas designated for our samples were selected from 2,025 such areas of the United States. Some sample areas represent only themselves and are referred to as self-representing. The remaining areas represent other areas similar in selected characteristics and are thus designated non-self-representing. The first-stage factor reduces the component of variation arising from sampling the non-self-representing areas.

4. *Second-Stage Adjustment.* This adjustment brings the estimates of the total population into agreement with census-based estimates of the civilian noninstitutionalized and nonbarrack military populations for each state.

B. Sportspersons Sample

Every interviewed person in the sportspersons detailed sample received a weight that was the product of the following factors:

1. *Screening Weight.* This is the person's final weight from the screening sample.

2. *Sportspersons Stratum Adjustment.* This factor inflates the weights of persons selected for the detailed sample to account for the subsampling done within each sportsperson stratum.

3. *Sportspersons Noninterview Adjustment.* This factor adjusts the weights of the interviewed sportspersons to account for sportspersons selected for the detailed sample for whom no interview was obtained. A person was considered a noninterview if he or she was not interviewed in the third wave of interviewing.

4. *Sportspersons Ratio Adjustment Factor.* This is a ratio adjustment of the detailed sample to the screening sample within the sportspersons sampling strata. This adjustment brings the population estimates of persons aged 16 years old and older from the detailed sample into agreement with the same estimates from the screening sample, which was a much larger sample.

C. Wildlife-Watchers Sample

Every interviewed person in the wildlife-watchers detailed sample received a weight that was the product of the following factors:

1. *Screening Weight.* This is the person's final weight from the screening sample.

2. *Wildlife-Watchers Stratum Adjustment.* This factor inflates the weights of persons selected for the detailed sample to account for the subsampling done within each wildlife watcher stratum.

3. *Wildlife-Watchers Noninterview Adjustment.* This factor adjusts the weights of the interviewed wildlife-watching participants to account for wildlife watchers selected for the detailed sample for whom no interview was obtained. A person was considered a noninterview if he or she was not interviewed in the third wave of interviewing.

4. *Wildlife-Watchers Ratio Adjustment Factor.* This is a ratio adjustment of the detailed sample to the screening sample within the wildlife-watchers sampling strata. This adjustment brings the population estimates of persons aged 16 years old and older from the detailed sample into agreement with the same estimates from the screening sample, which was a much larger sample.

ACCURACY OF THE ESTIMATES

A sample survey estimate has two types of error: sampling and nonsampling. The accuracy of an estimate depends on both types of error. The nature of the sampling error is known given the survey design; the full extent of the nonsampling error is unknown.

NONSAMPLING ERROR

For a given estimator, the difference between the estimate that would result if the sample were to include the entire population and the true population value being estimated is known as nonsampling error. There are several sources of nonsampling error that may occur during the development or execution of the survey. It can occur because of circumstances created by the interviewer, the respondent, the survey instrument, or the way the data are collected and processed. For example, errors could occur because:

- The interviewer records the wrong answer, the respondent provides incorrect information, the respondent estimates the requested information, or an unclear survey question is misunderstood by the respondent (measurement error).

- Some individuals who should have been included in the survey frame were missed (coverage error).

- Responses are not collected from all those in the sample or the respondent is unwilling to provide information (nonresponse error).

- Values are estimated imprecisely for missing data (imputation error).

- Forms may be lost; data may be incorrectly keyed, coded, or recoded, etc. (processing error).

The Census Bureau employs quality control procedures throughout the production process, including the overall design of surveys, the wording of questions, the review of the work of interviewers and coders, and the statistical review of reports to minimize these errors. Two types of nonsampling error that can be examined to a limited extent are nonresponse and undercoverage.

Nonresponse. The effect of nonresponse cannot be measured directly, but one indication of its potential effect is the nonresponse rate. For the FHWAR screener interview in Texas, the household-level nonresponse rate was **28** percent. The person-level nonresponse rate for the detailed sportsperson interview in Texas was an additional **20** percent and for the wildlife watchers it was **26** percent. Since the screener nonresponse rate is a household-level rate and the detailed interview nonresponse rate is a person-level rate, we cannot combine these rates to derive an overall nonresponse rate. Since the screener nonresponse rate is a household-level rate and the detailed interview nonresponse rate is a person-level rate, we cannot combine these rates to derive an overall nonresponse rate. Since it is unlikely the nonresponding households to the FHWAR have the same number of persons as the households successfully interviewed, combining these rates would result in an overestimate of the "true" person-level overall nonresponse rate for the detailed interviews.

Coverage. Overall screener undercoverage is estimated to be about 13 percent. Ratio estimation to independent population controls, as described previously, partially corrects for the bias due to survey undercoverage. However, biases exist in the estimates to the extent that missed persons in missed households or missed persons in interviewed households have different characteristics from those of interviewed persons in the same age group.

Comparability of Data. Data obtained from the 2011 FHWAR and other sources are not entirely comparable. This results from differences in interviewer training and experience and in differing survey processes. This is an example of nonsampling variability not reflected in the standard errors. Therefore, caution should be used when comparing results from different sources. (See Appendix C.)

A Nonsampling Error Warning. Since the full extent of the nonsampling error is unknown, one should be particularly careful when interpreting results based on small differences between estimates. The Census Bureau recommends that

data users incorporate information about nonsampling errors into their analyses, as nonsampling error could impact the conclusions drawn from the results. Caution should also be used when interpreting results based on a relatively small number of cases. Summary measures (such as medians and percentage distributions) probably do not reveal useful information when computed on a subpopulation smaller than 90,000 for screener data, 100,000 for the detailed sportsperson data, and 235,000 for the wildlife-watchers data.

SAMPLING ERROR

Since the FHWAR estimates come from a sample, they may differ from figures from an enumeration of the entire population using the same questionnaires, instructions, and enumerators. For a given estimator, the difference between an estimate based on a sample and the estimate that would result if the sample were to include the entire population is known as sampling error. Standard errors, as calculated by methods described in "Standard Errors and Their Use," are primarily measures of the magnitude of sampling error. However, they may include some nonsampling error.

Standard Errors and Their Use. The sample estimate and its standard error enable one to construct a confidence interval. A confidence interval is a range that has a known probability of including the average result of all possible samples. For example, if all possible samples were surveyed under essentially the same general conditions and using the same sample design, and if an estimate and its standard error were calculated from each sample, then approximately 95 percent of the intervals from 1.96 standard errors below the estimate to 1.96 standard errors above the estimate would include the average result of all possible samples. A particular confidence interval may or may not contain the average estimate derived from all possible samples. However, one can say with specified confidence that the interval includes the average estimate calculated from all possible samples. Standard errors may also be used to perform hypothesis testing, a procedure for distinguishing between population parameters using sample estimates. The most common type of hypothesis is that the population parameters are different. An example would be comparing the proportion of

anglers to the proportion of hunters. Tests may be performed at various levels of significance. A significance level is the probability of concluding that the characteristics are different when, in fact, they are the same. For example, to conclude that two characteristics are different at the 0.05 level of significance, the absolute value of the estimated difference between characteristics must be greater than or equal to 1.96 times the standard error of the difference. This report uses 95-percent confidence intervals and 0.05 level of significance to determine statistical validity. Consult standard statistical textbooks for alternative criteria.

Estimating Standard Errors. The Census Bureau uses replication methods to estimate the standard errors of FHWAR estimates. These methods primarily measure the magnitude of sampling error. However, they do measure some effects of nonsampling error as well. They do not measure systematic biases in the data associated with nonsampling error. Bias is the average over all possible samples of the differences between the sample estimates and the true value.

Generalized Variance Parameters. While it is possible to compute and present an estimate of the standard error based on the survey data for each estimate in a report, there are a number of reasons why this is not done. A presentation of the individual standard errors would be of limited use, since one could not possibly predict all of the combinations of results that may be of interest to data users. Additionally, data users have access to FHWAR microdata files, and it is impossible to compute in advance the standard error for every estimate one might obtain from those data sets. Moreover, variance estimates are based on sample data and have variances of their own. Therefore, some methods of stabilizing these estimates of variance, for example, by generalizing or averaging over time, may be used to improve their reliability. Experience has shown that certain groups of estimates have similar relationships between their variances and expected values. Modeling or generalizing may provide more stable variance estimates by taking advantage of these similarities. The generalized variance function is a simple model that expresses the variance as a function of the expected value of the survey estimate. The parameters of the generalized variance function are estimated using direct replicate variances. These generalized variance parameters provide a relatively easy method to obtain approximate standard errors for numerous characteristics. Table D-2 provide the generalized variance parameters for FHWAR data. Methods for using the parameters to calculate standard errors of various estimates are given in the next sections.

Standard Errors of Estimated Numbers. The approximate standard error, s_x, of an estimated number shown in this report can be obtained using the following formulas Formula (1) is used to calculate the standard errors of levels of sportspersons, anglers, and wildlife watchers.

$$s_x = \sqrt{ax^2 + bx} \tag{1}$$

Here, x is the size of the estimate and a and b are the param ters in the tables ass ciated with the particular characteristic

Formula (2) is used for tandard rrors of ggregates, i.e , trips, days, and expenditures

$$s_x = \sqrt{ax^2 + bx + \frac{cx^2}{y}} \tag{2}$$

Here, x is again the size of the estimate; y is the base of the estimate; and a, b, and c are the parameters in the tables associ ated with the particular characteristic.

Illustration of the Computation of the Standard Error of an Estimated Number

Suppose there were an estimated 37,397,000 persons age 16 years old and older who either fished or hunted in the United States in 2011. Using formula (1) with the parameters $a = -0.000070$ and $b = 16,823$ from table D-2, the approximate standard error of th estimat d number of 37,397,000 sportsperson age 16 years ol and older is

$$s_x = \sqrt{-0.000070 * 37,397,000^2 + 16,823 * 37,397,000} = 728,857$$

The 95-percent confidence interval for the estimated number of sportspersons 16 years old and older is from 35,968,000 to 38,826,000, i.e., 37,397,000 ± 1.96 x 728,857. Therefore, a conclusion that the average estimate derived from all possible samples lies within a range computed in this way would be correct for roughly 95 percent of all possible samples.

Suppose there were an estimated 13,674,000 hunters age 16 years old and older who engaged in 281,884,000 days of partici pation in 2011. Using formula (2) with the parameters $a = -0.000284$, $b = -127,863$, and $c = 46,699$ from table D 2, the approximate standard error on 281,884,000 estimated days on an estimated base of 13,674,000 hunters is

$$s_x = \sqrt{-0.000284 * 281,884,000^2 - 127,863 * 281,884,000 + \frac{46,699 * 281,884,000^2}{13,674,000}} = 14,586,000$$

The 95-percent confidence interval on the estimate of 281,884,000 days is from 253,295,000 to 310,473,000, i.e., 281,884,000 ± 1.96 x 14,586,000. Again, a conclusion that the average estimate derived from all possible samples lies within a range computed in this way would be correct for roughly 95 percent of all possible samples.

Standard Errors of Estimated Percentages. The reliability of an estimated percentage, computed using sample data for both numerator and denominator, depends on the size of the percentage and its base. Estimated percentages are relatively more reliable than the corresponding estimates of the numerators of the percentages, particularly if the percentages are 50 percent or more. When the numerator and the denominator of the percentage are in different categories, use the parameter in the tables indicated by the numerator.

The approximate standard error, $s_{x,p}$, can be obtained by use of the formula

$$s_{x,p} = \sqrt{\frac{bp(100 - p)}{x}} \tag{3}$$

Here, x is the total number of sportspersons, hunters, etc., which is the base of the percentage; p is the percentage; and b is the parameter in the tables associated with the characteristic in the numerator of the percentage.

Illustration of the Computation of the Standard Error of an Estimated Percentage

Suppose there were an estimated 13,674,000 hunters age 16 years old and older of whom 18.9 percent hunted migratory birds. From table D-2, the appropriate b parameter is 15,798. Using formula (3), the approximate standard error on the estimate of 18.9 percent is

$$s_{x,p} = \sqrt{\frac{15{,}798 * 18.9 * (100 - 18.9)}{13{,}674{,}000}} = 1.33$$

Consequently, the 95 percent confidence interval for the estimate percentage of migratory bird hunters 16 years old and older is from 16.3 percent to 21.5 percent, i.e. $18.9 \pm 1.96 \times 1.33$.

Standard Error of a Difference The standard error of the difference between two sample estimates is approximately equal to

$$s_{x-y} = \sqrt{s_x^2 + s_y^2} \tag{4}$$

where s_x and s_y are the standard errors of the estimates x and y. The estimates can be numbers, percentages ratios etc. This will represent the actual standard error quite accurately for the difference between estimates of the same characteristic in two different areas or for the difference between separate and uncorrelated characteristics in the same area. However if there is a high positive (negative) correlation between the two characteristics, the formula will overestimate (underestimate) the true standard error

Illustration of the Computation of the Standard Error of a Difference

Suppose there were an estimated 13,608,000 females in the age range of 18-24 of whom 726,000 or 5.3 percent were sportspersons. Similarly, suppose there were an estimated 12,909,000 males in the same age range of whom 2,160,000 or 16.7 percent were sportspersons. The apparent difference between the percentage of female and male sportspersons is 11.4 percent. Using formula (3) and the appropriate b parameter from table D 2 the approximate standard errors of 5.3 percent and 16.7 percent are 0.79 and 1.35, respectively. Using formula (4), the approximate standard error of the estimated difference of 11.4 percent is

$$s_{x-y} = \sqrt{0.79^2 + 1.35^2} = 1.56$$

The 95-percent confidence interval on the difference between 18 to 24 year-old female and male sportspersons is from 8.3 to 14.5, i.e. $11.4 \pm 1.96 \times 1.56$. Since the interval does not contain zero we can conclude with 95 percent confidence that the percentage of 18 to 24 year-old female sportspersons is less than the percentage of 18 to 24-year old male sportspersons.

Standard Errors of Estimated Averages Certain mean values for sportspersons, anglers etc. shown in the report were calculated as the ratio of two numbers. For example, average days per angler is calculated as

$$\frac{x}{y} = \frac{total \ days}{total \ anglers}$$

Standard errors for these averages may be approximated by the use of formula (5) below.

$$s_{x/y} = \frac{x}{y} \sqrt{\left[\frac{s_x}{x}\right]^2 + \left[\frac{s_y}{y}\right]^2 - 2r\frac{s_x s_y}{xy}} \tag{5}$$

In formula (5), r represents the correlation coefficient between the numerator and the denominator of the estimate. In the above formula, use 0.7 as an estimate of r.

Illustration of the Computation of the Standard Error of an Estimated Average

Suppose that the estimated number of the average days per angler age 16 years old and older for all fishing was 16.7 days. Using formulas (1) and (2) above, we compute the standard error on total days, 553,841,000, and total anglers, 33,112,000, to be 20,329,124 and 693,033, respectively. The approximate standard error on the estimated average of 16.7 days is

$$s_{x/y} = \frac{553{,}841{,}000}{33{,}112{,}000} \sqrt{\left[\frac{20{,}329{,}124}{553{,}841{,}000}\right]^2 + \left[\frac{693{,}033}{33{,}112{,}000}\right]^2 - 2 * 0.7 \frac{20{,}329{,}124 * 693{,}033}{553{,}841{,}000 * 33{,}112{,}000}} = 0.45$$

Therefore, the 95-percent confidence interval on the estimated average of 16.7 days is from 15.8 to 17.6, i.e., $16.7 \pm 1.96 \times 0.45$.

Table D-1. Approximate Standard Errors for Texas State Resident Anglers, Hunters, and Away-from-Home Wildlife Watchers

(Numbers in thousands)

Resident anglers, hunters, and away-from-home wildlife watchers	Estimate	Standard error
Resident Anglers		
Participation	2,355	251
Spenders[1]	2,079	238
Days of fishing	34,710	12,568
Expenditures in dollars	1,711,265	451,117
Resident Hunters		
Participation	1,080	148
Spenders[1]	1,036	145
Days of hunting	19,848	7,946
Expenditures in dollars	1,696,128	601,706
Resident Away-from-Home Wildlife Watchers		
Participation	977	158
Spenders[1]	879	150
Days away-from-home wildlife watching	11,193	4,487
Trip-related expenditures in dollars	335,013	117,313

[1] The spenders estimate for resident anglers and resident hunters is all participants who bought equipment and trip-related items The spenders estimate for away-from-home wildlife watchers is all participants who bought trip-related items

Table D-2. Parameters a, b, and c for Calculating Approximate Standard Errors for U.S. and Texas Screener, Detailed Sportsperson, and Wildlife-Watching Samples for Levels, Expenditures, and Days or Trips

Sample	Parameters					
	United States			Texas		
	a	b	c	a	b	c
Screener Sample						
Sportspersons, anglers, hunters, and wildlife-watching participants 6 years old and older	−0 000043	12,272	(X)	−0 000807	18,178	(X)
Sportspersons, anglers, hunters, and wildlife-watching participants 6 to 15 years old	−0 000387	15,783	(X)	−0 004712	18,120	(X)
Detailed Sportsperson Sample						
Sportspersons and anglers 16 years old and older	−0 000070	16,823	(X)	−0 001644	30,704	(X)
Hunters 16 years old and older	−0 000066	15,798	(X)	−0 001150	21,490	(X)
Expenditures for sportspersons and anglers 16 years old and older	0 001159	−575,615	45,670	0 049244	−64,415	42,177
Expenditures for hunters 16 years old and older	0 001923	−978,460	44,416	0 077228	−819,919	50,873
Days or trips for sportspersons and anglers 16 years old and older	0 000068	−160,414	51,951	0 114686	−85,855	44,518
Days or trips for hunters 16 years old and older	−0 000284	−127,863	46,699	0 128279	−71,291	38,430
Wildlife-Watching Sample						
Levels of wildlife-watching—away-from-home participants	−0 000134	32,078	(X)	−0 001436	26,817	(X)
Levels of wildlife-watching—wildlife-watching participants[1]	−0 000119	28,477	(X)	−0 001909	35,657	(X)
Expenditures for wildlife-watching	0 001308	−1,548,024	112,362	0 072728	−140,319	44,225
Days or trips for wildlife-watching	0 002307	826,023	54,100	0 058100	−1,079,923	206,159

(X) Not applicable

[1] Use these parameters for total wildlife-watching participants and around-the-home participants

U.S. Department of the Interior
U.S. Fish & Wildlife Service

http://wsfrprograms.fws.gov

May 2013